D1718497

SMART CARDS

John McCrindle

IFS Ltd, UK
Springer-Verlag
Berlin · Heidelberg · New York
London · Paris · Tokyo

British Library Cataloguing in Publication Data

McCrindle, John
  Smart cards.
  1. Smart cards
  I. Title
  004.56

ISBN 1-85423-001-8 IFS Publications
ISBN 3-540-512 56-X Springer-Verlag Berlin Heidelberg New York Tokyo
ISBN 0-387-512 56-X Springer-Verlag New York Heidelberg Berlin Tokyo

Phototypeset by Fotographics (Bedford) Ltd
Printed by Short Run Press Ltd, Exeter

Smart Cards

IFS

Dedicated to my wife Jennie
and children
Mary and Michael

Preface

It is little more than forty years since the first computers were produced. These machines each filled a room, weighed tens of tons, contained numerous parts and hundreds of miles of wiring. Little did people realise at that time that one day computers would be reduced in size to less than a square centimetre, be manufactured in millions, be embedded in plastic cards and be able to be carried around by every one of us. A computer in your pocket, costing only a few pounds was then only in the minds of the science fiction writer. Today such an idea has become a reality with the advent of the smart card – a computer in a plastic credit card type package.

As a portable, very secure, low cost, 'intelligent' device, capable of solving mathematical problems and manipulating and storing data, this small piece of plastic only 0.76 mm thick, containing a microcomputer, has all of the attributes to make it suitable for a wide range of applications. Already the smart card is in use for telephone call payment, satellite television access, storing medical data, car parking payment, military personnel records, financial transactions, identity and many other applications. Some of the applications for which the smart card is being used and will be used require only tens of cards, others require many millions. As the potential of the card is becoming known, trials and real applications are springing up around the world, in countries as far apart as France, Japan, New Zealand, and the USA. Despite the application of smart cards in these and many other countries, the technology is still only at 'the tip of the iceberg' in its growth cycle. It has all the qualities to become one of the biggest commercial products in quantity terms this decade as its potential becomes fully recognised.

In writing this book I have endeavoured to cover a broad spectrum of the subject in a manner which I hope will be understandable by the non-technologist. The book has been written to appeal to as many people as possible, to give them an insight into the technology and to illustrate how the smart card can be applied to the benefit of a business, service organisation and an individual, alike. It is from the ranks of the doctors, administrators, bankers, etc., that the drive to apply the technology will come as much as from the technological fraternity. It is therefore to these people as well as to the technologist that I hope this book will be of use.

The book itself can be considered to be in two parts. The first part addresses the technology: fundamental elements of the smart card, types of card, manufacturing process, etc. The second part, from chapter 8 onwards, is aimed at giving the reader an insight into many of the applications of the technology. In order to do this information has been included from a multiplicity of sources as well as from first hand knowledge. In making use of material from technical journals, newspers, etc., I apologise for any inaccuracies that I have perpetuated from the original articles. A glossary of commonly used terms and of useful addresses of suppliers and some users of the technology completes the book.

To conclude, I would like to thank a number of people in contributing help and for their comments. In particular I am indebted to Deidre Hollingum and Jack Hollingum who worked closely with me in producing this book and who helped carry out much of the hard work of putting my knowledge of the subject on paper. I would also particularly like to thank Chris Stanford for a number of useful comments on the draft manuscript and for some of the material on the GEC Smart Card. My thanks also to Tony Kirkman for his helpful suggestions; to Rick Jarvis, Dave Sylvester and Neil McDonald for comments on specific chapters of the book and to Sandra Debenham and Eileen Brandon for typing assistance. Also my thanks to Brian Rooks, Editorial Director at IFS Publications for his patience in awaiting the completion of the book and to GEC Avery Ltd for permission to publish the book. Last but not least my thanks go to my wife Jennie and children Mary and Michael for their patience and tolerance during the time I spent working on the book rather than spending my time with them.

Chelmsford, March 1990   John A. McCrindle

Contents

1 INTRODUCTION

SMART CARDS are likely to appear on a mass scale worldwide in the next ten years and will affect many areas of our lives.

What is a smart card? To someone accustomed to carrying a credit card or a bank card, a smart card may appear no different. It is the same shape as a conventional plastic card. It may even be embossed and have a magnetic stripe on the back. However, the appearance is deceptive because the smart card is not just another bank card but a new generation of portable computer.

Embedded in the card is a microcomputer chip giving it intelligence and a memory capacity far beyond that of today's magnetic stripe cards. It has as much computing power as the personal computers of the early 1980s.

The computer as we know it today has quite a short history, dating from the late 1940s. The first computers were the size of a room, had only a few dedicated applications, cost an enormous amount of money and the number built could be counted in tens. By the early 1980s a quite powerful computer could fit on a small desk. They were widely used, in large numbers, in industry, commerce and other areas. With prices ranging down to £100 they came within the budget of some households and began to appear in the home.

The smart card is the next step forward, as shown in Fig. 1.1. It is a computer which can be used in many applications, allows many people to afford it, at a price of £5, and is small enough to be carried around at all times – truly a computer in your pocket.

Like other computers the smart card can be programmed to do any task within its processing power and memory capacity. Its practical applications can be divided into three broad categories:

- *Data carrier*. Here the card is used as a convenient, portable and secure means of storing information; for example, medical records or equipment maintenance records.
- *Identification*. Here the card provides a secure means of identifying the holder so as to allow access to, say, a computer or a football stadium.
- *Financial*. The card can be used for transactions as a replacement for cheques or pensions, for example.

Some applications fit into more than one of these categories. For instance, a smart card acting as a train season ticket would provide both identification at the ticket barrier, or on the journey, and financial payment for the journey.

In addition, the card is not restricted to a single application. It could contain emergency medical data relating to the cardholder (data carrier), provide a means of gaining access to a building where the person works (identification), and be used in vending machines at the place of work (financial). Fig. 1.2 shows just a few of the many applications for which smart cards can be used. This is by no means a comprehensive list – applications are limited only by one's imagination.

MARKET POTENTIAL

Three examples may serve to give some idea of the vast potential market in each of the above categories.

Within 40 years the computer
has evolved from the size
of a room to the size
of a credit card

GEC Card Technology

Fig. 1.1 Within 40 years the computer has evolved from the size of a room to the size of a credit card. The Manchester University Mark I (top) ran the world's first stored program in 1948. (Top photograph courtesy of the National Archive for the History of Computing, PC photograph courtesy of SciTech Micro Systems).

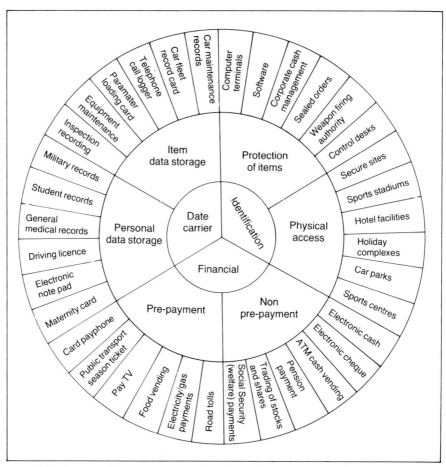

Fig. 1.2. Some of the many applications for smart cards

Data carrier

There is an increasing interest in the use of smart cards to store general medical records. The card could be carried by the individual and contain vital medical data relating to the cardholder, such as allergies and drugs being taken, which, in the event of an accident, might help to save a life. One can envisage, for example, that within the next ten years everyone in the UK will carry such a medical smart card – a card base in excess of 60 million. Will the cost of such a card be a deterrent? For some people it undoubtedly will be, but £5, for a plastic card which carries information that could save your life, would seem a good insurance policy.

Identification

Satellite television is an area now emerging as a major opportunity for smart cards. For a pay television service the card can be programmed to unlock the scrambled television signal. Early in 1989 the executive chairman of Sky Television, a new satellite channel serving the UK, announced that the company would be using smart cards. Manufacture was to begin in the autumn of 1989 and, within the first 12 months it was intended that at least two million cards would be produced. The chief executive was reported to have said, 'We will actually end up making more money out of smart cards than out of Sky Television, and we will make a lot of money out of Sky'.

Financial

Estimates vary, but there is a general view that the number of financial cards in circulation today, both banking and retail, is approximately one billion. Growth is of the order of 10% annually. If over the next ten years, only 10% of this card base is converted to smart cards then the number of smart cards in circulation will be in excess of 100 million.

The driving force for converting to smart cards is likely to be the ever-increasing level of fraud which the smart card is able to counteract. The ability of the smart card to carry out multiple functions is also very attractive. In the USA, it is estimated, the average card-carrying person has seven cards. The ability to incorporate many of these into one card will undoubtedly encourage card users to favour the smart card.

At first, adoption of the smart card will be restrained by its cost but prices will fall as the technology matures, leading to faster adoption and the benefits of high volume manufacture. Initially the card will penetrate areas where the price is not too critical. For instance, in the USA it is estimated that 18 million people are already paying over $50 for prestigious gold cards and the cost of a smart card will not be a restriction in this market.

INTERNATIONAL PROGRESS

A few years ago there was little interest in, or even knowledge of, smart cards. Today there is great interest worldwide, as shown in Fig. 1.3, and the amount of activity is steadily increasing. There are scores of trials under way throughout the world, in countries which range as widely as the USA, France, Japan, Norway, the UK and Senegal. The

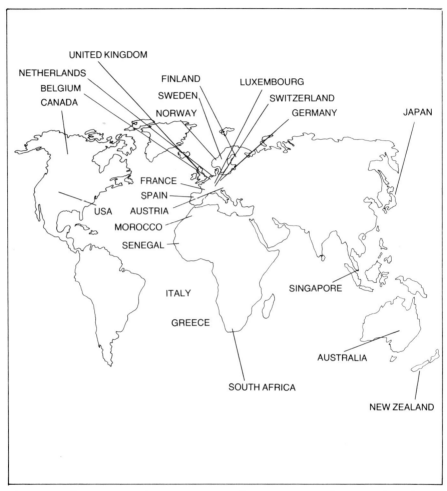

Fig. 1.3. Countries where smart card systems are being piloted and implemented

applications to which they are being put include storage of medical data, allowing access to leisure facilities, financial transactions, and monitoring vehicle fuel consumption.

The French, who did much of the pioneering work with this technology, still lead the way. In 1990 they intend that payments by smart card will be general all over France and they are now in the process of taking delivery of 16 million cards. Norway was forecasting that there would be over 550,000 smart cards issued in their country by the end of 1989. In the USA, the Department of Agriculture is using smart cards to help automate the paperwork-based system employed for the peanut harvest – more than 100,000 smart cards are in use for this application.

PURPOSE OF THIS BOOK

The smart card is on its way – but it is still some distance from achieving its enormous potential. The aim of this book is to provide sufficient information for the reader to gain a full understanding of the smart card and how it might be applied. It is written in non-technical language for the general reader, the banker, the doctor and so on, because it is these people, quite as much as the technologists, who will ensure the widespread adoption of smart cards.

After the historical introduction in Chapter 2 the book is in two parts. Chapters 3 to 7 cover the technical aspects, describing the fundamental elements of a smart card, the different types of smart cards and associated types of cards, the manufacture of cards and the security features which they offer.

Chapters 8 to 12 cover applications. Rather than dealing with them under the three broad categories listed above, it was thought more useful to divide them according to the four primary commercial and industrial areas where they are coming into use – with a fifth chapter covering the remaining important applications. So Chapters 8 to 11 deal, in turn, with financial, medical, leisure/travel and telecommunications applications, while Chapter 12 looks at a number of important applications in other areas which may emerge as even bigger markets than some of the primary areas.

Each of these chapters is divided into three. The first part gives a brief description of the chief uses of the card within the application area. This is followed by details of trials and schemes where smart cards are already in use. The third part takes one or two applications as case studies for detailed description.

By covering the applications in this way we hope the reader will gain a good understanding of where smart cards are likely to find successful applications, how to implement the technology, what problems have been encountered by others and what benefits can be expected.

Two of the case studies, describing medical and telecommunications implementations, relate to cards which should strictly be described as 'memory' cards rather than smart cards. They have been included because, in a world where practical experience is scarce, a great deal of experience has been gained with memory cards which would equally apply to smart cards. Indeed, in the case of the medical application, the original memory cards used in the first stages of the trial are now being upgraded to contactless smart cards.

To help the reader take the next step towards implementing the use of smart cards we include at the end of the book a list of useful addresses of companies associated with smart cards. There is also a glossary of commonly used terms.

2 EVOLUTION OF THE SMART CARD

THE EVOLUTION of the smart card is the story of two parallel product developments that were to merge into one product in the 1970s. The two products in question are the computer, or to be more specific a miniaturised computer – the microcomputer chip, and the magnetic stripe card.

THE MICROCOMPUTER CHIP

The history of the computer could be said to begin when man was first faced with performing calculations and recording data. Early forms of computing devices included the abacus which allowed calculations to be performed by moving beads on a frame of rods and wires according to a set of rules.

The first mechanical calculator is considered to have been the invention of a French philosopher, Blaise Pascal. The Pascaline, as his machine was known, could add and, if adjusted, subtract. It consisted of interlocking cogs and wheels on different axles. These rotated when a number was dialled and the result was shown in a small window.

In the early nineteenth century Babbage pushed the development of the computer forward with the invention of his 'Difference Engine'. This was designed to perform arithmetic calculations which were advanced enough to generate complex tables. His machine was partly built but never completed because engineers of the time were unable to make the machine to his specifications. It is now known, however, that the Difference Engine would have worked had engineering techniques been sufficiently advanced to allow it to be built. Babbage moved on to design another, more general purpose, machine called the 'Analytical Engine'. This machine, too, was not constructed but Babbage spent some time, until his death in 1871, considering design problems and making some of the parts.

A tabulating machine was used for the first time in the American census of 1890. Herman Hollerith and John Shaw Billings had the idea of using punched cards to mechanise the processing of data derived from the census.

Mechanical calculators continued to be improved and developed during the nineteenth and early twentieth centuries but it was not until the 1930s that the crucial step was taken to incorporate valves into what were still essentially mechanical machines. A team headed by Vannevar Bush, working at the Massachusetts Institute of Technology, invented the Differential Analyser having realised that using exclusively mechanical parts would impose considerable restrictions. Hence the team decided to use valves to store values as voltages. The resulting machine was very large but could carry out general purpose calculations.

The next important step in the development of the computer was taken by a German, Konrad Zuse, who made his first computer, the Z-1, in 1936. His second computer, the Z-2, was completed in 1939 and in this design he made the advance of using electromagnetic relays instead of mechanical switches is some sections. He describes his next computer, the Z-3, as 'the first program-controlled computer which worked as a complete entity'. It is unfortuante that only the improved version of the Z-3, which was designated Z-4, survived the Berlin air raids.

Meanwhile, in Britain work on computers was concentrated on producing a code-breaking machine. A team of top mathematicians and electronics experts were installed at Bletchley Park during the early years of the war and set to work. They developed a series of electromagnetic machines known as the Robinson series. This was followed by the Colossus series. The first of the Colossus machines used 2,000 valves and was completed in 1943. A paper tape provided the data input at a speed of 5,000 characters per second. In all, ten of these machines were built and they represented the first digital computers. They were much faster than any mechanical or electro-magnetic machines of the time but were limited in their scope as they had only been developed for a dedicated purpose.

The American company, IBM, started working seriously on the development of a general purpose computer at about the same time as Zuse invented the Z-1. The IBM project was led by Howard Aiken at Harvard University. He had looked again at Babbage's Analytical Engine and decided that a similar machine could be constructed with the technology now available. The result was a machine based on electromagnetic relays and called the Automatic Sequence Controlled Calculator (ASCC), better known as the Mark I. It was completed in 1944 and was 45ft. (14m) long, 8ft. (2.4m) high and contained 500 miles of wiring and 750,000 parts. Maintenance of the Mark I was, naturally, a problem but it was in use for 15 years.

The first completely electronic general purpose computer, shown in Fig. 2.1, was completed in 1945. It was the idea of John Mauchly and J. Presper Eckert, of the Moore School of Engineering, University of Pennsylvania, and it took three years to develop. The Electronic Numerical Integrator and Computer (ENIAC) weighed over 30 tons, occupied 1,500ft.^{2} (140m^2) of floor space, consisted of about 18,000 vacuum tubes, 70,000 resistors, 10,000 capacitors and 6,000 switches, and used 150kW of power. In theory it was programmable but reprogramming the machine was a difficult process requiring some rewiring. The ENIAC was used to produce ballistics tables and weather forecasts.

The idea of storing a program within the computer itself was conceived by John von Neumann who became a consultant for the team at Moore School in 1946. If this concept was possible then reprogramming would be less of a problem. In the event, however, it was Tom Kilburn and Frederick Williams, at Manchester University, who first managed to produce a computer with a stored program. In 1948 the Manchester Mark I computer, using a Williams storage tube, executed its first program. Maurice Wilkes, at Cambridge University, produced the EDSAC computer not long after and it was he who introduced the concept of microprogrammed architecture.

The first computer to be produced commercially was the Univac I, developed by Eckert and Mauchly at Remington Rand. Forty-eight of

Fig. 2.1. ENIAC was the first completely electronic general purpose computer, completed in 1945. (Photograph courtesy of the Moore School of Electrical Engineering, University of Pennsylvania)

these were made and the first one went to the USA Census Board in 1951.

By the early 1950s the basic foundations of computing had been laid. Over the next few years computers continued to be improved and the applications they were used for expanded. They were, however, still large, cumbersome machines and comparatively slow in operation. The move into microelectronics did not happen for another twenty years.

The work done by Michael Faraday and others, on electrical power and the development of the valve vacuum tube, had contributed greatly to the technological progress made during the early part of this century. However, valves were found to be unreliable and they used a large amount of power. Great efforts went into finding an alternative to the valve vacuum tube and, at the end of 1947, three men working at Bell Telephone Laboratories in the USA invented an alternative device known as the germanium point-contact transistor. John Bardeen, Walter Brattain and William Shockley were later awarded the Nobel Prize for Physics for their work on the transistor. During the early 1950s the transistor was developed to the point where it became possible to produce it commercially.

Electrical devices were becoming increasingly complex during the 1950s and connecting the components together into a circuit presented difficulties for manufacturers. The process was time consuming and labour intensive, so there was a need for a more streamlined method. The answer turned out to be the integrated circuit or chip as it became known. Two people, Jack Kilby, of Texas Instruments, and Robert Noyce, of Fairchild, have been independently credited with the invention of the chip.

A Japanese company, Busicon, provided the challenge, in the late 1960s, which led to the development of the microprocessor. The company asked Intel, a chip manufacturing company founded by Robert Noyce and others, to produce 12 chips for a new range of programmable calculators. Intel had been experimenting with a new microchip technology which made it possible to increase the number of transistors on a chip from 600-1,000 to 2,000 and the technicians believed that the Busicon calculators could be produced with fewer of these higher capacity chips.

The task of designing the chips for the Busicon calculators fell to Marcian Hoff who had worked with a Digital Equipment Corporation PDP-8 computer before joining Intel. His ideas, based on his experience with the PDP-8 computer and the new chip technology, led to the design of three chips. These comprised:

- The central processing unit (CPU) – the microprocessor.
- A read-only memory (ROM) for the program.
- A random access memory (RAM) for the data.

The number of ROM and RAM chips varied according to the type of calculator.

Busicon agreed to the design and work began on producing the chips. This was not an easy task and progress was slow at first. The design was changed from three chips to four, by the addition of a shift register chip, and the complete set was named the MCS-4. The microprocessor, known as the 4004, contained about 2,200 transistors. Busicon initially retained the sole right to market the chips but Intel later negotiated the right to sell the chips for other uses. The company's first advertisement for a microprocessor appeared in 1971.

Texas Instruments had shown that it was feasible to contain all the circuitry required for a microcomputer on one chip and they were awarded the patent in 1971. The first 8-bit single chip microcomputer was produced in 1976 by Intel. The chip was called the 8048 and consisted of a CPU, ROM, RAM and input/output. Later that year a version of the chip was produced which contained ROM that could be erased by ultraviolet light (EPROM).

By the end of 1976 chip technology had developed to a point where it would be possible to incorporate a chip into a plastic card to produce the early smart cards.

THE MAGNETIC STRIPE CARD

The other side of the story, the development of the card, could have its beginnings in the last years of the nineteenth century. The first mention of a credit card is believed to be in a book called *Looking Backwards* by James Bellamy, which was published in 1880. The credit card he talked about was an IOU or banker's credit facility which had to be combined with some form of identification.

By the 1920s the idea of a credit card was gaining popularity and, in the USA some retailers and petrol companies were issuing their own cards. These were made of cardboard and engraved to provide some security.

The 1930s saw the introduction of some embossed metal and plastic cards. The use of credit cards was increasing and it was becoming important for the information to be extracted from the card as quickly as possible. Embossed cards could be used to imprint information on to a sales voucher.

The following thirty years saw the market for credit cards expand rapidly. Banks became interested and started issuing cards in the 1940s. The retailing industry continued to be a particularly keen user of credit cards but new industries, such as the travel and entertainments industries, began to issue their own cards. Diners Club introduced its charge card in 1950 while the first American Express cards date from the end of the 1950s. In 1969 the first magnetic stripes were added to the embossed cards. It was not practical for magnetic stripe readers to be installed immediately in every place accepting credit cards so the embossing has remained.

The new magnetic stripe cards were used internationally and standards were needed to ensure that they could all be used worldwide. The International Standards Organisation (ISO) laid down standards covering various aspects of the cards including the dimensions, embossing and location of the magnetic stripe. These are still generally conformed to.

The magnetic stripe card was being used in many parts of the world by the mid-1970s. However, losses through fraud and bad debts were high. Both Visa and Mastercard were said to lose 1% of their gross sales each year. Most of the losses were due to bad debt although somewhat less than 15% was due to card-related crime. To counter this, security features such as holograms, fine background printing and signature panels were added to the cards. The banks have also introduced measures enabling them to identify an occurrence of fraud more quickly and, in addition, the legal penalties for card fraud have been strengthened.

THE MERGING OF THE MICROCOMPUTER CHIP AND CARD

Computers and magnetic stripe cards gradually began to come together as computers were used increasingly in processing card transactions. In 1974 Roland Moreno, a French journalist, had the idea of putting a chip inside a conventional plastic card. He patented his idea and founded a company, Innovatron, to promote it. In 1976 CII Honeywell Bull obtained a worldwide licence for the development of the card. Flonic Schlumberger followed suit in 1979 and in the same year Philips obtained a licence for France only. Smart Card International was the first US company to obtain a licence and today there are many companies which have been licensed by Innovatron to manufacture and sell smart cards.

Moreno was not, in fact, the first person to apply for patent protection for a plastic integrated circuit card. Dr Kunitaka Arimura of Japan had filed an application four years earlier for such a card, but his application covered Japan only. His patent was granted and all smart cards now made in Japan have to be licensed by his Arimura Institute.

Moreno's patent did not say how the goal of putting a computer into a card should be achieved an Innovatron's three licensees adopted different approaches to the problem. Schlumberger's approach was to aim for a low-cost card which could compete on the level of price and performance with a magnetic stripe card. The resulting card had hard-wired logic on a single custom-designed chip and, using this approach, Schlumberger was very soon able to meet the ISO standards for card thickness. This card has proved to be highly successful and, to date, Schlumberger is the world's largest single supplier of chip cards.

Both Honeywell Bull and Philips were aiming for a more complex card containing a microprocessor. Meeting the ISO requirements for financial magnetic card presented technical difficulties but, by 1979, Bull had produced prototype cards which had a Motorola micro-processor chip embedded in them and metallic contacts on the surface. At this stage the prototypes were thicker than the ISO standard. Within a short while the company announced its CP8 range of cards and, at the same time, stated its intention to produce a range of compatible readers for different applications, e.g. telephones and point-of-sale transactions. The Philips cards used Intel chips and larger memories, but neither system gave access to the memory for reprogramming, so the cards had to be discarded when the memory was full.

At this time, in France, the government was having to review the country's telephone system which was outdated and had become inefficient. To update the telephone system, the government embarked on a programme which included new schemes for electro-nic directories and videotext services. It was also intended that this programme, known as the 'Telematique Programme', should help revitalise the ailing French computer industry, and the development of smart card payment systems was to play a part in this.

By late 1981 both Bull and Philips had been able to reduce the thicknesses of their cards to meet the international standard of 0.76mm. This raised the interest of banks, because the cards could be used, during a transitional period, in the same automatic teller machines as existing magnetic stripe cards.

French banks saw that the introduction of videotext services across the country would open up the possibility of home shopping and banking to a far greater number of people. Hence they put investment into the development of smart cards and, in 1981, began trials in three cities (Lyon, Caen and Blois). The cards used in these trials were made by Honeywell Bull and Philips and had metallic contacts on the surface. The cards were powered through the contacts when inserted into the slot of a card reader. They were used much as ordinary credit cards except that they could record and authorise a transaction without having to be on-line to a central computer.

In 1982 and 1983 the French PTT (telephone company), with support from a government economic development programme, ran trials using smart cards with videotext and telephone directory terminals, known as Minitels. The cards were used to pay for telephone calls, control access to Minitels, control access to banking facilities and to record transactions. Each household had two or more smart cards carrying the identity and address of the cardholder and pre-loaded with a cash value. At the time, card readers delivered to the 300 homes involved in the trial were not a convenient size. Since then they have been improved and some Minitel models contain card readers.

In 1984 the French PTT ran a trial using smart cards with public telephones. The success of this trial encouraged them to think in terms of replacing up to one third of all 170,000 existing coin-operated public telephones with new ones, operated by smart cards. This replacement work commenced and is still continuing.

Interest in smart cards was beginning to grow in other countries by the early 1980s and in Japan, for example, a programme of smart card development and investment was under way.

Development was also taking place in a slightly different direction, with patents being filed for contactless smart cards. Work was being done on contactless cards in the USA, by AT&T, and in Britain, by GEC. The development of the GEC card had begun in 1982 at the Marconi Research Centre. The team at GEC had recognised the potential of smart cards but saw some disadvantages in using metallic surface contacts to power the card. GEC's intention was to produce a card which could be powered and could communicate without being inserted into a slot. The success of this early research work led to a new company, GEC Card Technology, being set up to manufacture and sell contactless smart cards.

In Japan and the USA some people were taking the smart card a stage further and designing the concept of a smart card with a display and keyboard. This concept became known as the super smart card.

In 1985 the ISO set up an international steering committee to look at the possibility of agreeing standards for contact smart cards. The standards were intended to cover such items as the contact position, interface protocol and information content and control.

Mastercard and Visa both announced smart card trials in the USA in 1985 and other trials were being run by medical insurance companies, the US Army and other organisations, such as the US Department of Agriculture.

Towards the end of 1985 the French banks made a decision to begin replacing all their magnetic stripe cards with smart cards. They negotiated orders for 12 million cards from Bull and four million from Philips. Largely because of pressure from the banks, Honeywell Bull and Philips had earlier agreed to manufacture compatible cards of the CP8 type, while continuing to compete in the market-place. This had resulted in more rapid banking industry developments led by the newly-formed 'Groupement Carte Bancaire' which was responsible for placing the order for 16 million smart cards known as the 'Carte Bancaire'.

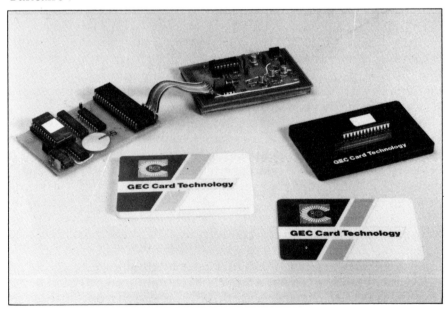

Fig. 2.2. Stages of card development that have led to an ISO standard GEC contactless smart card. From top to bottom: the printed circuit prototype comprising two boards; a 5mm thick card with a protruding EPROM which could be removed for reprogramming; a 5mm thick card which could be reprogrammed from the read/write unit; the ISO standard card. (Photograph courtesy of GEC)

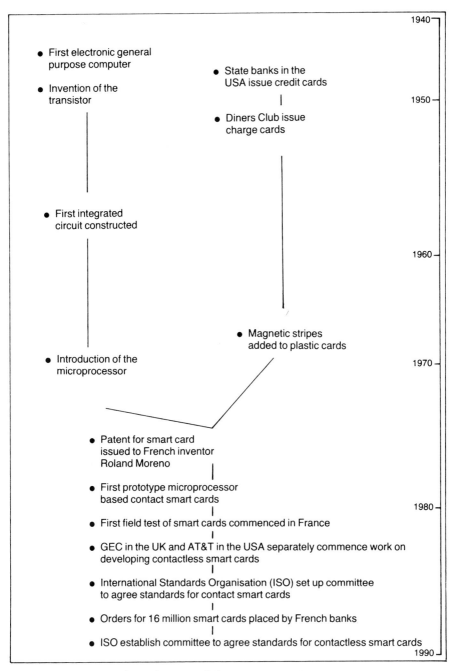

Fig. 2.3. Historical evolution of the smart card

Important trials are also under way using contactless smart cards. In a trial at an airport the contactless card, produced by AT&T, is being used with public telephones. The GEC card is involved in a trial, with Midland Bank at a British university, where it is being used as a multi-function card for financial payments and access to information terminals.

A working group established in 1989 to set the standards for these cards, under the auspices of the ISO, has confirmed that the contactless smart card has also come of age. The development stages of the GEC contactless card, leading to the ISO standard size version, are shown in Fig. 2.2 and the historical evolution of smart cards is summarised in Fig. 2.3.

We can look forward during the next decade to a rapid growth in smart card applications until the smart card truly becomes the computer in everyone's pocket.

3 FUNDAMENTAL ELEMENTS OF A SMART CARD

A S WE have said, a smart card is a computer. It differs from the normal concept of a computer only in the fact that it is generally available in a plastic credit card package, which makes it very portable, and it costs very little. Although there are a number of different types of smart cards they all have in common the same three fundamental elements as any other computer – processing power (the smart part), data storage elements and a means to input and output data.

The processing power is supplied by a microprocessor chip and the storage elements by a memory chip. Some cards have these combined on one chip (a microcomputer – also known as a microcontroller) as shown in Fig. 3.1, while others have them separated. The microprocessor incorporated in the card can differ from one card manufacturer to another, as can the type of memory. The means by which data is transferred in and out of the cards, and the units through which they communicate, can also be different. Although each element may differ

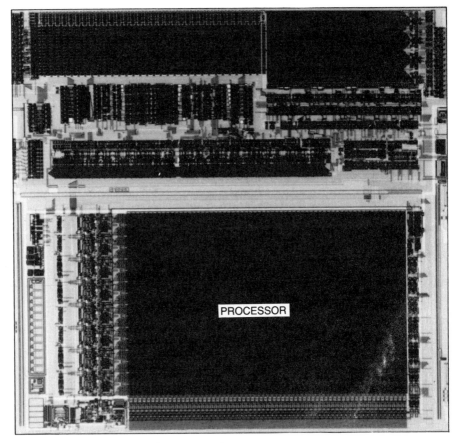

Fig. 3.1. Structure of a typical smart card microcomputer chip. (Photograph copyright by Oki Electric Ind. Co. Ltd)

in detail each performs the same basic tasks. Before the card can function it must have a source from which it can be powered.

MICROPROCESSOR

The microprocessor is the intelligent element of the smart card. It performs two basic functions: the manipulation and the interpretation of data. It carries out these functions by executing instructions stored in the card's memory. The set of instructions that can be executed by the microprocessor is called its instruction set and each instruction has a unique binary code* that can be interpreted by the microprocessor. For example: 10101101 means 'add'; 11101100 means 'subtract'; and 10101010 means 'store in memory'.

It is from such an instruction set that the sequence of instructions stored in memory, or *program* as it is known, is formed. There are two basic types of program – the *operating system* and the *application program*. The operating system comprises various groups of instructions, *routines*, which are not dependent on the particular application and will frequently be used in most applications; for example, an initialisation sequence, transmission and reception of data. The application program comprises the set of instructions that define the functions the card is to perform within a specific application, such as financial transactions or security identification. In some smart cards the operating system and application program are closely merged and a distinction cannot be drawn between the two. Like the program, data is also stored in memory in the form of binary codes.

The microprocessor can read the contents of a memory location or write data to a given location, when it executes the appropriate instruction in its program. The stored data can be a representation of some value or event external to the microprocessor; for example, a binary number could be allocated to each letter of the alphabet.

The program and data are known as *software*. Both can either be embedded in the memory during manufacture or input under control of the microprocessor, dependent upon the system employed by each card manufacturer.

Microprocessors are often classified according to the number of bits which they are capable of manipulating simultaneously. This number defines the basic resolution of the microprocessor. For example, a 4-bit microprocessor will perform all calculations on binary numbers with four bits, an 8-bit microprocessor will perform all calculations on binary numbers of eight bits, and so on. Typically, smart cards have 8-bit microprocessors.

---

* Digital computers carry out all their storage and manipulation of data by means of electrical charges held in sets of locations. Each charge can be either present or absent so that it represents a binary digit, or 'bit'. The word 'binary' is used of a counting system consisting only of the digits 0 and 1, forming a sequence 0, 1, 10, 11, 100, 101, 110 and so on. A set of eight binary locations allows eight-figure binary numbers to be represented, for example 10110110. The eight-figure binary number is called a 'byte' and contains 2^8 or 256 binary numbers which could, for example, represent decimal numbers from 0 to 255.

MEMORY

Memory is made up of an array of cells. The cells have two electrical charge states, charge present and charge absent, which represent the binary numbers 1 and 0. It is from these two binary digits that the instructions and data are formed in memory. Typical memories used in smart cards have capacities of 8,192† (8k) bits, 16,384 (16k) bits and 65,536 (64k) bits. The memory is usually organised in 'bytes' of 8-bit lengths. So an 8kbit memory is often referred to as a 1kbyte memory, a 16kbit memory as a 2kbyte memory and a 64kbit memory as an 8kbyte memory.

All memories exhibit one of two characteristics. Either they retain data after the power source is switched off, or data is lost when the power source is removed. The former is called *non-volatile memory*, the latter *volatile memory*. They also fall into one of two other categories. In one case data can be written into the memory and also read from the memory. In the other case data can only be read from memory – it cannot be written to memory. Smart card applications usually require at least some of the memory to be both non-volatile and read/writable. The card has to be non-volatile to retain information such as the name of the cardholder and the application software. It also has to be writable so that it can be updated to store information such as the balance after a transaction has been made.

The memory used in smart cards can be divided into three types:

● Read Only Memory (ROM).
● Random Access Memory (RAM).
● Programmable Read Only Memory (PROM).

ROM is a non-volatile memory, the contents of which are embedded in the chip at the chip manufacturing stage. Once embedded the contents cannot be altered. RAM, on the other hand, is a volatile memory. When power is not applied the data stored in this type of memory is lost. Its main characteristic is that data can be written to it, deleted, altered in any way and read from it. As its name suggests its memory can be accessed in random order, although this is also true of other types of memory. RAM is generally used in smart card systems as a temporary storage area.

---

† The somewhat confusing method of counting used in describing computer memories is the result of mixing binary and decimal arithmetic. A kilobit, or kbit, is not 1,000 bits but 2^{10} or 1,024 bits. Similarly, a kilobyte (kbyte) is 1,024 bytes and a megabyte (Mbyte) is 1,048,576 bytes.

	In card programming	In card erasing	Data retention when power removed	Relative cell area
ROM	Not programmable	Not erasable	Date retained	1
RAM	Re-programmable	Erasable	Data lost	20
EPROM	One-/time programmable	Not erasable	Date retained	2
E² PROM	Re-programmable	Erasable	Data retained	4

Fig. 3.2. Comparison of memory types

Unlike ROM, which is non-volatile but is not reprogrammable, and RAM, which is reprogrammable but volatile, PROM is both non-volatile and reprogrammable. There are two principal types of PROM – *electrically programmable read only memory* (EPROM) and *electrically erasable programmable read only memory* (EEPROM, also called E²PROM). Characteristics of the different types of memory are summarised in Fig. 3.2.

EPROMs have been available for a number of years and it is a well-proven technology. Initially, all memory cells are in the 1 state. During programming certain cells will be changed to the 0 state. The disadvantage of EPROM technology is that the programmed memory cells cannot be reprogrammed, back to a 1, electrically. To change the contents of memory the entire memory has to be erased and this can only be achieved by exposing the device to ultraviolet light. When incorporated in an electronic circuit the EPROM chips are usually mounted in a ceramic package with a quartz window which will allow ultraviolet light to reach the chip. This type of packaging is, obviously, not suitable for smart cards. EPROM is therefore used in smart card applications that allow the card to be disposed of after all EPROM locations have been programmed, or where the EPROM memory contents do not need to be changed more than once.

As its name suggests, *electrically erasable programmable read only memory* (EEPROM), which is a more recently developed technology than EPROM, can be reprogrammed by electrical means and does not need to be exposed to ultraviolet light. This means that it can be packaged without the need for a transparent window. Another significant advantage of EEPROM is that it is not necessary to erase the entire memory, as each memory cell can be reprogrammed individually. One of the disadvantages of EEPROM is that the technology is based on a two-transistor structure rather than the single transistor structure of EPROM. This has the effect of increasing the chips area which makes it more expensive than an EPROM with equivalent memory capacity and more susceptible to cracking when the card in which it is embedded is flexed. This is discussed more fully in the chapter on manufacturing.

The mechanisms for programming EPROM and EEPROM are quite different. A significant current is required to program an EPROM cell whereas only a low current is needed to program an EEPROM cell. An EPROM may take one milliamp per bit to program while an EEPROM may require less than one microamp. As a result of the low current requirement of EEPROM, circuits may be incorporated on the chip to generate the high voltage necessary to program the device. This is not possible with EPROM because of the high current requirements. A consequence of this is that it is not possible to utilise EPROM in a contactless card because there is a limit on the power that can be transmitted to the device. EEPROM, on the other hand, can be used in both contact and contactless cards.

Smart card memory structures

The types of memories discussed earlier, i.e. ROM, RAM, EPROM and EEPROM, can be configured for use in different ways within a smart card. Three of the more common types of structures are shown in Fig. 3.3.

Fig. 3.3(a) shows the structure of a card containing ROM, EPROM and RAM. A general purpose programme is stored in ROM. The program is embedded in the ROM during the manufacturing process and is known in the electronics industry as customising or masking the ROM. This process is described in more detail in a later chapter. Once customised the ROM cannot be altered. The EPROM is used for storage of data under control of the software program in ROM. Once each location has been programmed it cannot be changed, so when the memory is full the card has to be thrown away. The RAM is used as temporary storage for intermediate calculations.

Fig. 3.3(b) shows the memory structure of a card which has EEPROM memory. The ROM usually contains the operating system with general purpose utility programs. As discussed previously, these programs could include: routines for transferring data via a read/write

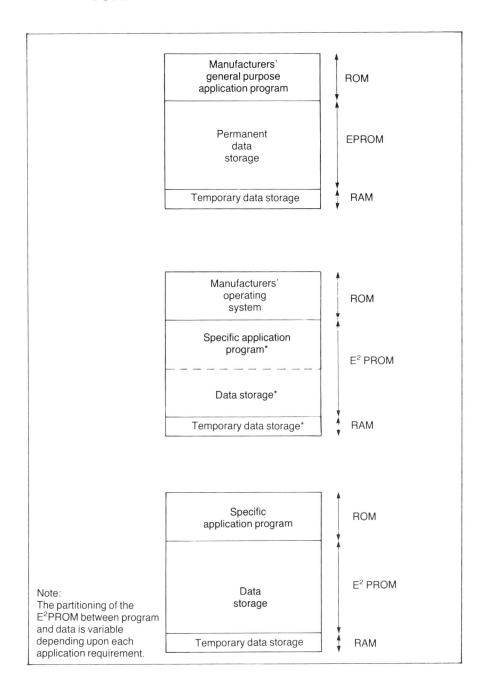

Fig. 3.3. Smart card memory structures

unit, into the card and out from the card, to an external device; encryption routines and other general purpose software.

The EEPROM memory contains the application program and an area for data that has to be retained when the power is removed from the card. This can usually be partitioned by the user according to the size of the required application program and the amount of memory space required for data. As in the previous example the RAM is used for temporary storage.

In the third example, Fig 3.3(c), the application program is stored in the ROM and the EEPROM is used for data storage only. The cost of having the ROM customised is not cheap so this structure is only likely to be used in applications where the cost can be amortised over a large number of cards and where there is no likelihood of change to the application program. Storing the application program in the ROM does, however, have the advantage of giving the user maximum space for data storage. The RAM is again used for temporary storage.

Open, working and secret zones

Various ways of structuring the memory to provide a hierarchy of security zones, are employed by different card suppliers. There are, however, three fundamental zones: open, working and secret. The *open* zone contains information which is not confidential, such as the cardholder's name and address. It can be read by the card reader but alterations cannot be made by an unauthorised person.

The *working* zone contains confidential information. Certain information must be given to the card before access is permitted. The most usual way of presenting this information to the card is by inserting the card into a reader, with the cardholder entering a personal identification number (PIN). For financial applications the confidential information could be, say, the amount of a purchase, the date and details of the merchant from whom the purchase was made. Also contained here would be the information that the card's microprocessor checks before authorising a transaction, such as the available credit and the number of transactions that can be allowed in a defined period.

In the *secret* zone the information is completely confidential. The contents are not accessible to the cardholder and need not be known in total by the issuer or the manufacturer. This zone holds data such as the PIN. The card's microprocessor has access to this zone and can examine the PIN and compare it with the PIN entered by the cardholder via a keyboard. This ensures that the PIN never leaves the card, thereby maintaining a high level of security.

INPUT/OUTPUT

For the smart card to be of any use it must be able to interact with the 'outside world'. Therefore, it must have a means by which it can receive and send data. The method varies, depending upon the type of card. Some cards for instance, communicate through metallic contacts on the card's surface while others do so by the contactless transmission and reception of data. Others communicate via a keyboard and display incorporated in the card.

All but the last type of card can only operate when used in conjunction with a read/write unit. In the case of the card with metallic contacts, it has to be placed into a slot in the read/write unit and, in doing so, a link is made with a connector inside the unit. Through this connector data can flow both into and out of the card. Some contactless cards have merely to be placed on or near the surface of the unit for data to be transmitted and received.

Unlike other types of cards, a card with integral keyboard and display can operate as a stand-alone device, data being input by depressing the keys and memory contents read on the display by depressing other keys. These cards also often incorporate contacts to facilitate the fast transfer of information with other electronics-based devices. Detailed explanations of input/output features of the various types of cards are given in the next chapter.

Read/write units with which the cards communicate can be categorised into four basic types which are described in the following list. The choice of read/write unit is dependent upon the system or product into which it is to be incorporated.

Intelligent stand-alone units

These units each contain a processor, memory, keyboard, display and all the functions necessary to perform tasks without being connected to other units.

Non-intelligent units

These read/write units do no more than provide the interface between the card and another device, such as a computer. The read/write unit acts as the receptacle in which the card is placed or sits and carries out any signal and data format conversions that are necessary for there to be a 'conversation' between card and computer. The read/write unit generally has a standard interface, RS232 for example, to allow it to be connected to a range of computers and other devices.

Fig. 3.4. Portable contact smart card read/write unit. It is battery powered although it can also be powered from the mains. (Photograph courtesy of Bull CP8)

Hand-held read/write units

These low-cost units are small, can be held in the hand, are battery powered and usually contain a keyboard and small display. (see Fig. 3.4).

Integral read/write unit

An integral read/write unit is usually a basic non-intelligent unit which has been embedded in a larger, more complex device, such as an automatic teller machine (ATM).

POWER SOURCE

There are three principal methods currently in use for powering a smart card:

- From an external power source feeding current through contacts on the card.
- By transmitting power.
- By a battery embedded in the card.

The first method is applicable to cards with metallic contacts on the surface of the card (see Fig. 3.5(a)). Two of the contacts are designated as the power rails and power is sent through them to the microelectronics when the card is placed in a read/write unit. The card, which had been dormant, will then 'wake up' and after being reset will commence the execution of its operating system or application program.

The second method, shown in Fig. 3.5(b), is applicable to contactless cards. Methods used for contactless operation, such as inductive coupling, allow both data and power to be transmitted from the read/write unit through the air or a non-metallic surface to the card. This is covered in more detail in a later section on contactless operation.

A third method of powering a smart card is to incorporate a battery in the card, as in Fig. 3.5(c). Batteries can often be found as a power source in smart cards that are thicker than the size laid down by ISO standards. They are mostly found in smart cards which contain only RAM technology as the memory medium, requiring the battery to maintain the contents of the RAM when the card is not in contact with a read/write unit, and in cards which incorporate keyboards and displays.

Today very thin batteries are available which can have relatively long lives, sometimes up to five years, and it has become practical to incorporate them in cards. In general, however, this is not a popular option. Unpopularity is due to the difficulty of incorporating the battery within the card thickness dimensions laid down by the ISO, problems associated with flexing a card containing a battery; and the additional cost incurred in incorporating a battery.

Some thin card calculators use solar cells on the surface to provide sufficient power for the device to operate but this method for powering a smart card is currently not popular because of its limitations:

- It requires good ambient light.
- Cells are vulnerable to breakage when the card is flexed.
- It is more costly than cards which obtain power through contacts or via contactless operation.

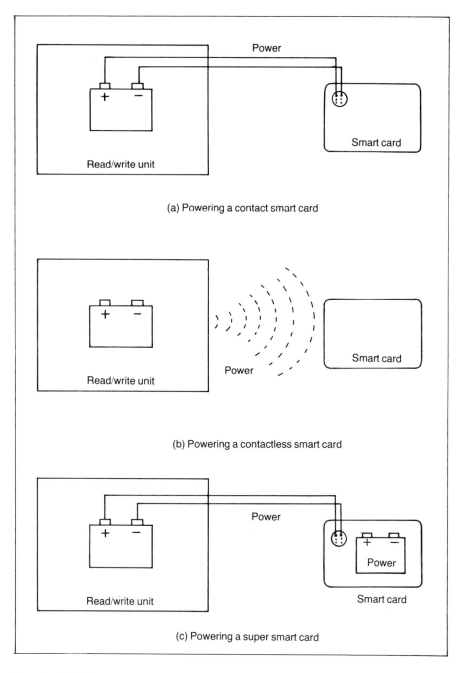

Fig. 3.5. Different methods of powering a smart card

4 TYPES OF SMART CARDS

IN THE last chapter we discussed the fundamental elements that are found in all smart cards – the microprocessor, memory and input/output. There is a variety of smart cards available from a number of different manufacturers. They can vary in terms of the microprocessor used, the type of memory and the way they communicate with the read/write unit. However, they can be broadly divided into the three different categories illustrated in Fig. 4.1 – contact cards, contactless cards and super smart cards (cards with an integral keyboard and display). This chapter examines each category in turn and gives details of specific cards.

The term 'smart card' is often used in a broad sense to include cards which contain large amounts of memory, but have no intelligence, and tags which can communicate over relatively long distances. For the purpose of this chapter, smart cards will be defined as devices that have both processing power and memory, and are capable of being

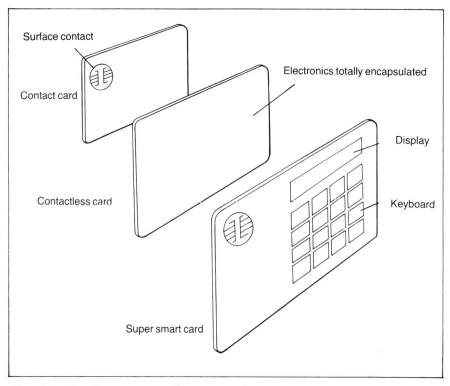

Surface contact

Electronics totally encapsulated

Contact card

Display

Contactless card

Keyboard

Super smart card

Fig. 4.1. The three types of smart cards

packaged in the format laid down by the ISO. 'Capable' is the operative word here. The electronic core of, for instance, a contactless card which has been re-packaged in a key fob or dog tag format is still considered to be a smart card. For completeness other devices, such as memory cards which are closely associated with smart cards, are covered in the next chapter.

CONTACT SMART CARDS

Smart cards with surface contacts were the first type to reach the market-place. Currently, there are more of these cards in use than any other type. The 16 million smart cards being issued in France at the moment are all of the contact variety.

Contact smart cards have the microelectronics embedded in the card with connections to metallic contact pads on the surface of the card. The contacts are the link by which the read/write unit and the card's microcomputer communicate and the means by which power is fed to the microelectronics. There are eight contacts, as shown in Fig. 4.2, and the allocation of the function of each has been standardised. Two of the contacts are reserved for supply voltage and ground (zero voltage reference), one for reset and one for the clock signal which provides timing information for the microprocessor to carry out its operational sequences. The remaining contacts provide for serial data input and output, and the supply of power necessary to program the memory while two are reserved for future allocation.

The card layout, in particular with respect to the position of the chips, was finally standardised by the ISO in the autumn of 1987, after a great deal of international lobbying. The French had been manufacturing contact smart cards for several years and were interested in having the contact position on their cards – the top left-hand corner – adopted as the standard. Manufacturers from other countries would not accept this because it could interfere with the magnetic stripe on the back of the card. Also, the Japanese have the magnetic stripe on the front of the card and this too would have clashed with the French contact position.

Eventually it was agreed that the standard position for the contact should be in the left centre part of the card on either the front or back. The standard allows the previous contact position, as used by the French and others, to be used during the transition period up to 1990.

As with many other types of smart cards, contact cards generally incorporate a magnetic stripe for compatibility of use with existing equipment, and they can also be embossed.

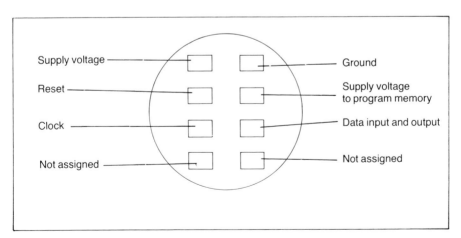

Fig. 4.2. Contact cards have eight interface contacts

The Bull CP8 card

The CP8 (see Fig. 4.3), an acronym for 'portable computer in the '80s', has been the core product of Bull, which has pioneered the work on smart cards. The CP8 contains a single chip incorporating an 8-bit microprocessor and memory. Although an EEPROM version has now come into use, the CP8 has primarily been an EPROM-based card. In use the card's EPROM is available for application-specific data. Versions of the card containing 8kbits, 16kbits and 64kbits of EPROM are produced by Bull. As well as having EPROM, the chip embedded within the card has a small amount of RAM, for use as temporary storage memory, and ROM. The ROM contains a set of programs that define the functions of the card etched in during manufacture by *masking*, as it is known. Bull offers several standard mask options and is prepared to develop masks on request for specific applications. The principal standard masks that the company offers are:

● *M4 Mask*. This is currently the most widely used in banking applications in France and in a number of other countries. The M4 mask enables the EPROM memory to be segmented into security areas, data areas and a fabrication area. Access to these areas can be restricted according to the degree of confidentiality of the information they contain.

Fig. 4.3. Bull CP8 contact smart card. (Photograph courtesy of Bull)

- *M9 Mask*. This is very similar to the M4 mask but is the mask used for higher memory capacity cards.
- *MP Mask*. The MP (multi-purpose) mask has been developed to allow a number of totally independent services to co-exist on the same card, so that the card may have more than one main issuer.

Information between the card and read/write unit is transmitted at 9,600 bits per second (a bit per second is often referred to as a baud).

The fabrication area mentioned above is a free reading zone which cannot be added to once the card is personalised. It contains information such as:

- Pointers to the start of the various areas of memory.
- Access protection rules.
- The card serial number defined during manufacture.

CONTACTLESS SMART CARDS

Contactless technology is defined as a means of transferring data between a smart card and a read/write device that does not require the use of external contacts. This can take place through a number of different technologies.

One of the technologies used in powering contactless cards is *inductive coupling*. This is used extensively in power transfer, particularly in AC circuits. Familiar domestic electrical equipment, such as stereos and televisions, use transformers which operate on the principle of inductive coupling. The coupling process involves the use of two coils of wire, one acting as the primary coil the other as the secondary coil. When an alternating current is passed through the primary coil an alternating magnetic field is created. When the secondary coil is brought in close proximity to the primary coil the alternating magnetic field induces a flow of current in the secondary coil.

Altering the system so that a current alternating at two different frequencies, representing binary 1 and binary 0, is passed through the primary coil, means that data can be transmitted to the secondary coil. This method of transferring data is referred to as *frequency modulation* or *frequency shift keying*. The receiving side, which could be the smart card, demodulates the signal and retrieves the data at the same time as it uses the transmitted power to activate its circuitry. In the same system the sending side, incorporating the primary coil, would be the read/write unit. Inductive coupling has, therefore, the advantage of being able to transfer both information and power to a smart card.

The transfer of data from the smart card to the read/write unit can be done in other ways. One approach uses amplitude modulation, where the alternating signal being sent is varied in amplitude between two levels, one level representing a binary 1, the other representing a binary 0. This technique is used in the GEC intelligent contactless (iC̄) card described later in this chapter.

Capacitive coupling is yet another way of transferring data to and from a read/write unit and a smart card. If a pair of conductors are placed just below the surface of the smart card, and a voltage signal is placed across them, then a charge separation which generates an electric field is formed between the plates. The electric field can extend beyond the surface and can induce another charge separation on a second pair of conductors in the read-write unit. Using this technique, data can be transmitted between the card and read/write unit.

The advantage of capacitive coupling is that digital information can be transferred directly and, unlike the inductive coupling technique which uses AC current, no modulation is required. The ones and zeros of the digital information can be imposed directly across the capacitor plates.

The AT&T card, described in detail later, uses this approach. The card has four capacitor plates in its circuit configuration – two are used for data transmission and two for data reception. The read/write unit has similar plates for communications with the card.

Other possible methods for non-contact communication include microwave coupling, optical coupling and surface acoustic wave coupling, but the methods described previously remain the most common in use for smart cards.

Contactless smart cards offer a number of advantages over contact cards and these are discussed below. However, it should be borne in mind that not all of the advantages are applicable to all contactless cards, some of which have to be inserted in slots or precisely aligned on the read/write unit. Benefits include:

- *Reliability*. In any electrical system contacts are almost invariably the points where failures occur. A contactless interface makes the card intrinsically more reliable than cards with surface contacts which are susceptible to damage, contamination and wear.
- *Longer life*. A potentially longer life; for the reasons mentioned above.

- *Facility*. In use the contactless card can be placed in any orientation on the read/write unit, even upside down. It is easier and faster to use than a contact card which has to be placed in a slot.
- *Convenience*. The read/write unit can be mounted under or behind any non-metallic working surface. This is very useful in banks and at retailing check-outs, keeping counters free of equipment.
- *Minimal maintenance*. Unlike many conventional card reading mechanisms the read/write units have no moving mechanical parts.
- *Vandalism-proof*. In most cases the read/write units have no slots that in conventional readers are often subject to vandalism; for example, by putting glue or chewing gum in the slot.
- *Robustness*. Read/write units can withstand harsh environments. They can be made available as fully-sealed electronic units. The contactless card and read/write unit are most suitable for working in industrial or other harsh environments where either may become covered with oil, water, grease or dirt. These conditions could cause major problems for cards with exposed surface contacts and read/write units with slots.

The GEC intelligent contactless (iC) card

Various contactless smart cards are now emerging, and the GEC smart card shown in Fig. 4.4 is one of the leaders. The GEC smart card was designed with the following set of objectives in mind:

- No physical connection necessary between the card and read/write unit for the card to operate.
- Read/write unit to be insensitive to card orientation.
- Slotless operation, with the card able to operate a small distance away from the surface of the read/write unit.

These objectives are achieved by inductive coupling between coils embedded in the card and read/write unit. The two coils perform the functions of transferring power to the card, transferring data to the card and transferring data from the card.

An oscillator, controlled by a crystal, pulses a tuned circuit, in the read/write unit, or coupler as is is known. The signal is received by the tuned circuit in the card and is processed (rectified and regulated) to provide the card's circuitry with DC power. The card uses the frequency of the power field as a stable reference to generate the microcomputer's clock which is at a much higher frequency. As mentioned previously, a clock is used to control the timing of

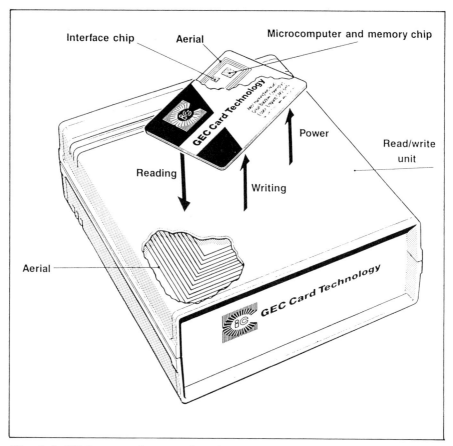

Fig. 4.4. GEC contactless card and read/write unit. (Diagram courtesy of GEC)

operations performed by the microcomputer.

Data is sent to the card by frequency modulating the power field. The frequency of the power field is determined by the data input to the coupler and the card uses a decoder to recover it. Data is transferred from the card to the coupler using amplitude modulation. Circuitry in the card causes a switching on or off of a part of the circuit depending on the logic state of the data being sent from the card. This has the effect of the card drawing more or less power from the coupler. The coupler detects changes in amplitude of the power field and its circuitry converts the changes back into data. The data rate, programmed from the card's software, can be anything from 300 to 9,600 bits per second.

The interface functions of the card are performed by one relatively small chip which carries out:

- Rectification.
- Regulation.
- Clock generation.
- Frequency decoding.
- Switching.

The chip interfaces directly with the card's microcomputer chip. The interface chip also connects directly with the loop aerial assembly which is the coil that couples into the power field. The loop aerial assembly also forms the substrate on which the interface and microcomputer chips are mounted before encapsulation to form the finished card.

The 8-bit microcomputer contains both memory and processor on one chip. Any data leaving this device for the interface chip prior to transmission can be sent in encrypted form. Thus, security is maintained as there is no question of probing between the two devices and extracting meaningful information. The current version of ISO card contains 5kbytes (40kbits) of memory. This is partitioned into 3kbytes of ROM and 2kbytes of EEPROM. There are also 128 bytes of RAM for temporary data storage.

An 8kbytes (64kbits) version of the card, which is 5mm thick, is also available. The entire memory in this card is RAM, the contents of which are maintained by a battery when the card is not operating with the coupler. The memory can be partitioned between the application program and data as the user likes, although 1kbyte is reserved for the card's operating system which controls the loading of application programs, data transmission and other functions.

The coupler comprises two boards: the aerial board and the electronics board. The aerial board consists of a power stage and a tuned aerial coil. The reason for the aerial being designed as a separate module is that the geometry of the assembly may vary according to the application. The maximum distance over which the card and reader can communicate is determined by coil geometry and input power, but is typically 20mm. The electronics board is the same for every application and contains the frequency reference, frequency modulator and amplitude modulation detector, as well as providing a serial RS-232 data input and output. It has two additional control signals – one detects the presence of the card on the coupler and the other allows the card to be externally reset. The entire assembly is powered by a single 12V DC power supply.

In addition to its credit card format the GEC iC card is also produced in key fob, dog tag and other formats.

The Valvo contactless chip card (C2-card)

A different type of contactless card is produced by Valvo, a subsidiary of Philips. This contactless chip card, as shown in Fig. 4.5, and known as the C2-card, also uses induction as the means for data transfer and for powering its microelectronics. Unlike the GEC iC card it has two inductive coils and works when placed in a slot in the read/write unit rather than on the surface of the unit. The two coils allow the card to work when inserted either way up. The card contains three chips: an 8-bit microcomputer, an EEPROM memory and an interface chip known as the CCI (contactless chipcard interface). The output lines from the chip are the same as those laid down by the ISO standards for contact cards. This means that the standard smart card chips now being produced by a number of chip manufacturers can be used in the card.

Toppan contactless card

In July 1988 it was reported that a Japanese company – Toppan Printing Company Ltd. – had produced a contactless smart card with length

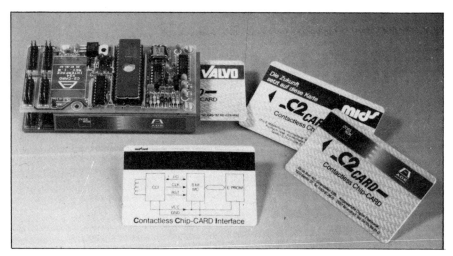

Fig. 4.5. Valvo contactless chip C2-card and read/write unit. (Photograph courtesy of Valvo)

and width the same as a standard card but with a thickness of 3mm. This card operates using three induction coils in the card and three in the read/write unit. One set, consisting of one coil in the card and one coil in the read/write unit, is used for power transfer and the clock. Another set is used for data input and the third set for data output. Unlike many other smart cards, the Toppan card has separate lines for data input and output, making simultaneous transmission and reception possible. To see how the card operates refer to Fig. 4.6. Coils L1 and L3 have the same specification and driving circuit performance. These coils are located symmetrically about the centre of the card in the longitudinal direction, allowing the card to function irrespective of whether it is inserted face up or down in the read/write unit. L1, L2 and L3 coils in the read/write unit are directly opposite coils L1*, L2* and L3* in the card. The frequency of the clock, which is transferred through the card's L3* coil together with power, is divided in half, processed and sent back through the L2* coil to the read/write unit, (see Fig. 4.6(a)). When the signal is received by the read/write unit it assumes that the card is in the proper position. L1 acts as the data transmitter to the card, L2 acts as the data receiver from the card, and L3 continues to provide the power and the clock (see Fig. 4.6(b). If, on the other hand, the card is inserted the other way round, such that L1* and L3* coils are in reverse position, the halved clock frequency does not get back to the read/write unit, as in Fig. 4.6(c). In this case switching takes place in the read/write unit, as in Fig. 4.6(d), making the L1 coil work as if it were the L3 coil and *vice versa*. The card then functions as normal (see Fig. 4.6(e)).

AT&T contactless smart card

The AT&T card illustrated in Fig. 4.7 is an example of a card which employs two forms of contactless technology in one card – inductive and capacitive. As with the previous cards that have been described, an inductive coil is used to power the card. However, this is not the means by which data is transmitted. Four capacitor plates are part of the card's circuit configuration, two each associated with data transmission and reception. The read/write unit has a similar set of plates for performing the communication task. When data is transmitted to the card it goes into an analogue interface chip. This restores the data to a clean form for the microcomputer, conditions the power and restores the clock required by the microcomputer.

One of the limitations of using capacitive coupling is that the card has to be more precisely aligned on the reader for data transmission

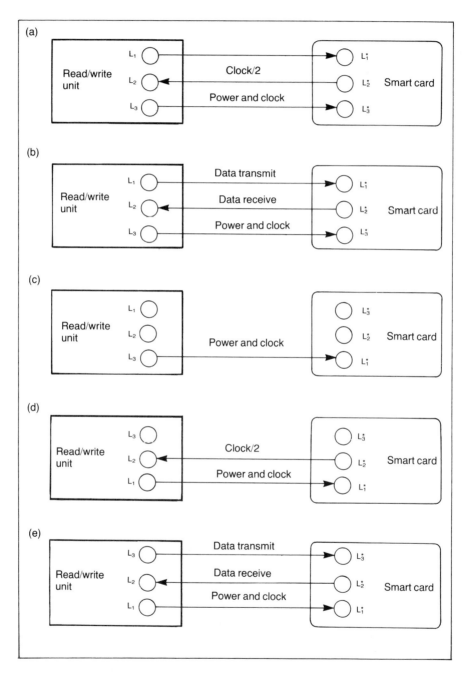

Fig. 4.6. Principle of operation of the Toppan contactless card

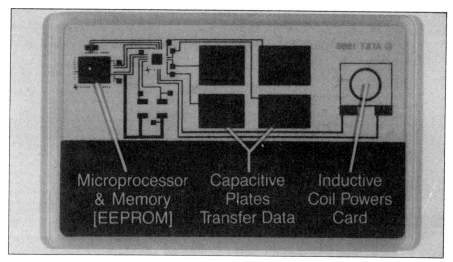

Fig. 4.7. Internal structure of the AT&T contactless smart card, which uses inductive and capacitive technologies. (Diagram courtesy of AT&T)

and reception than a card using inductive coupling. Data can be transmitted or received at speeds of up to 19.2kbits per second. As with the GEC iC card the card contains an 8-bit microprocessor and EEPROM memory integrated into a single chip. The product is available in three different packages: in a card format, a military-type tag and as an identity badge. All products share the common AT&T contactless technology for physical design, electrical design and software design.

SUPER SMART CARDS

The super smart card is the third category of smart card. It differs from the other smart cards quite radically insofar as it incorporates a keyboard and liquid crystal display (LCD). It can function more like a stand-alone terminal without the need of a card read/write unit. Although it can work independently there are occasions when it needs to go on-line, for instance to a computer. To accommodate this function these cards also, generally, have surface contacts. To maintain downward compatibility with magnetic stripe readers the card is able to emulate, electronically, a magnetic stripe being read. As with other cards, a logo and an embossed cardholder's name and number can be incorporated. In the case of the super smart card, on the side of the card, opposite the display and keyboard. The driving force for the development of the super smart card has come, very much, from Visa International. Working with the Toshiba Corporation of Japan, Visa brought the card into existence, although another company involved with this technology is Smart Card International of New York.

Visa super smart card

Many of the components of the Visa super smart card shown in Fig. 4.8 were developed especially for the card. They were implemented in very high density CMOS technology which has the advantage of requiring low power. One of the large-scale ICs contained in the card has an 8-bit microprocessor, 16kbytes of ROM and 8kbytes of RAM.

Serial communication to a card reading device is carried out via the electrical contacts (in the ISO position) by a receiver/transmitter circuit. Surge absorbers, connected to the contacts, protect the components inside the card from damage by static electricity. The

Fig. 4.8. Visa super smart card. (Photograph courtesy of Visa International)

other components of the card include a real time clock and calendar and an interface to the keyboard. Crystal oscillators provide timing signals to both the real time clock and the microcomputer.

Like other smart cards, the Visa super smart card needs to be compatible with magnetic stripe card readers. During development it was decided to incorporate a magnetic-head transducer which could emulate the signals of a normal magnetic stripe card but with the added capability of being able to emulate different magnetic stripe entries for different accounts. Since then a magnetic stripe has also been added to the card, giving a still wider choice of functions.

The LCD is 16 segments wide, each segment comprising of a 5 by 7 dot matrix. Dot patterns for the character fonts are contained in a display driver. The card contains two thin, paper lithium batteries which provide the power for the RAM so that data can be retained. The batteries also power the display. They can produce 3V for approximately three years with average use.

The need to keep the card within ISO standard thickness for plastic cards compelled Toshiba to develop a number of new manufacturing techniques. With so many electronic components packed into the card it would have been impossible to use conventional embossing techniques without running the risk of seriously damaging the card. Hence, a new technique was developed by Toshiba which does not involve heat or pressure. During the manufacturing process, clear plastic pads are formed on the front panel of the card. The issuing bank then uses a computer numerically controlled (CNC) engraving unit to mill the pads into the required alphanumeric characters showing, for instance, the cardholder's name and card number.

The internal components are packaged between two sheets of stainless steel, with a stainless steel spacer to separate them. The edges are fused together by a laser. The super smart card does not flex to the same extent as a conventional plastic card but it should be able to withstand the amount of bending it would receive in normal use. It also has to withstand the pressure put on it by sales slip imprinting devices.

The Visa super smart card is intended to be used as a multi-function card without necessarily requiring an external read/write unit. The functions available to the cardholder, at present, include financial services, clock and calendar, electronic notepad and calculator. The cardholder has a PIN which must be entered before access to the financial services and electronic notepad can be granted.

When making a purchase with the card, the cardholder has to enter the PIN and the amount of the purchase. The balance in the account is then checked and the purchase deducted from it and stored in the card. The LCD screen then displays a unique approval code which the retailer can trust as confirmation that the card transaction is valid.

The card has been designed for use either in card-accepting machines, such as ATMs, or manually through the keyboard. The card is activated in a card-reading machine when it senses electrical activity at the chip contacts. When used manually, the card is activated by the cardholder pressing the 'yes' key. The card then displays the time and date alternately and the cardholder can choose to enter a financial service, reset the time or calendar, look at or change the notepad, or perform a calculation. The card can also perform currency conversions using an exchange rate programmed by the bank before the traveller leaves for his destination. If he presses the 'no' key while the card is displaying the time and date the card will be switched off.

It is possible for the card issuer to add to the functions available on the card. In a trial in Japan, for instance, the super smart card is being used to dial telephone numbers automatically and to pay for ticket reservations over the telephone.

The main disadvantages of the super smart card are its much higher cost in comparison with other smart cards, the difficulty in meeting ISO flexing and other standards, and the small size of the keypad which makes it slow in use.

5 OTHER TYPES OF CARDS

IN THE last chapter we discussed the various types of smart card. In addition to these cards there are a number of other, closely associated, devices, some of which are often referred to as smart cards. They basically fall into two categories either side of true smart cards – see Fig. 5.1.

In one of the categories falls a group of devices which are basically memory cards – that is, they have no on-board computing ability but have memories of various capacities. At the bottom end of the scale is the forerunner of the smart card – the magnetic stripe card with a memory capacity of less than 250bytes. At the top end of the scale is the optical card with a memory capacity of 2,000,000bytes (2Mbytes). In between are cards which incorporate chips and have various memory capacities. A fourth group is tags which started out as tracking devices attached to objects or people. They contained very little memory but could transmit and receive information over

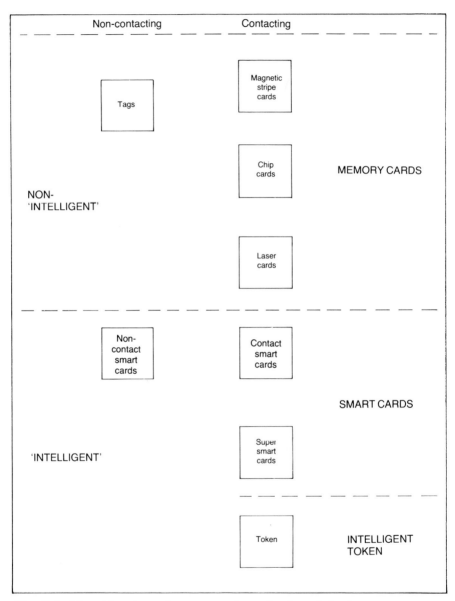

Fig. 5.1. Classification of smart cards and related devices

relatively large distances, of the order of metres. They are increasingly containing more memory and, more importantly, some are incorporating computing ability.

The second category of device is that of the intelligent token – a device which, in the foreseeable future, is unlikely to be smaller than a pocket calculator but which has a lot of processing power.

This chapter will briefly describe each of these 'other types of cards' and give a brief summary of the principal applications for which they are used.

MAGNETIC STRIPE CARDS

Magnetic stripes began to be used on plastic cards largely as a result of the move towards automation in the banking industry. There had been increases in the number of customers using the banks and in the range of services that were being offered. This left banks with a choice between automation or costly expansion involving increased staffing levels and the acquisition of more bank premises. ATMs were seen as a way of speeding up some bank transactions and plastic financial transaction cards, bearing a magnetic stripe, were introduced to operate these machines. The introduction of ATMs began in the late 1970s and the number of machines in use grew to 170,000 by 1985.

Although magnetic stripe technology has been in existence for many years, it was not used widely with financial transaction cards until the late 1970s. One of the factors which delayed the adoption of magnetic stripes was the time it took for international standards, covering the layout and reading requirements of the cards, to be agreed and published by the ISO.

The magnetic stripe card is manufactured in the same way as any other plastic card, consisting of layers of laminated plastic. The magnetic stripe is a strip of magnetic tape similar to that used for audio recording. There are two methods by which it may be applied to the card. In one method, known as the Franklin method, it is stamped on to the finished card. The other method is the lamination method in which the stripe is plated on the outside of the layers to be laminated and is laminated with them.

The magnetic stripe allows data to be recorded via an appropriate read/write device. The string of magnetically-recorded data bits can be read back sequentially at a later time by the reader head. Modern magnetic stripes have been divided into three tracks which are designated for different applications. The ISO standard numbers the tracks according to their proximity to the card's top edge, track 1 being the track nearest to the top.

Track 1

This track was developed by the International Air Transportation Association (IATA) and holds alphanumeric information for the issue of airline tickets when a reservation database is accessed. Track 1 has a recording density of 210 bits per inch, each character is 7 bits long and the track has an information content of 79 alphanumeric characters.

Track 2

The American Bankers Association (ABA) developed this track, normally referred to as the banking industry track. It contains numeric information for use with automatic financial transactions. This track is used by most systems requiring identification numbers. It has a recording density of 75 bits per inch, each character is 5 bits long and the track has an information content of 40 numeric characters. Track 2 is written before the cardholder receives the card. When the card is used with an on-line terminal it is interrogated and the information concerning the cardholder's account and identification are transferred to the card issuer's central computer to be checked.

Track 3

This track was developed by the Thrift Industry and contains information which is intended to be updated with each transaction. It is used with off-line cash dispensers. Track 3 has a recording density of 210 bits per inch, each character is 5 bits long and the track has an information content of 107 numeric characters. The third track was developed after the others and it is the only one that can be rewritten. It usually contains an encoded version of the cardholder's PIN. When the cardholder enters his PIN it is compared with the PIN encoded in the magnetic stripe without reference to a central computer. This eliminates the need to transmit data to a distant computer for confirmation before the transaction can proceed.

Other features

The capacity of the magnetic stripe limits the number of new features that can be introduced. The maximum number of characters is 226, if all the tracks are full. Various suggestions have been made for increasing the capacity of the magnetic stripe, to give more space for banking information and increase the services offered by a magnetic stripe financial transaction card. Some of the features incorporated on a modern magnetic stripe card are shown in Fig. 5.2.

Security is a problem with magnetic stripe cards because the card is passive and cannot check the validity of either the cardholder or the terminal it is presented to. Devices for reading and changing data held on magnetic stripes are not difficult to obtain and this increases the security risk. However, there are ways in which this kind of forgery can be made more difficult. One solution is the use of a high coercivity magnetic stripe. This type of stripe requires a much greater magnetic

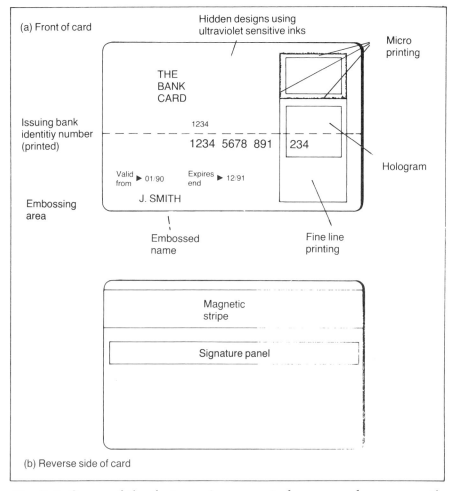

Fig. 5.2. Some of the features incorporated on a modern magnetic stripe card

field for encoding than the normal magnetic stripe and, thereby, gives a higher level of security. While high coercivity magnetic stripe cards are now being used as prepaid telephone cards, they are not yet in use for financial applications.

Another security technique, developed by EMI/Malco, includes the card's unique serial number on the magnetic stripe in a machine readable form. The number on the stripe must match the number on the card before the machine will accept it. This technique is known as the 'watermark'.

There are drawbacks to using magnetic stripe cards but the magnetic stripe does have some advantages over the newer smart card. It is, for instance, very much cheaper to produce – even after the hologram was added as a security feature, the price per card was still less than $1. Additionally, a large investment has been made in magnetic stripe cards, and appropriate terminals, and much of the equipment in use is still relatively new with even more being installed. It is, therefore, unlikely that major card issuers will suddenly completely abandon magnetic stripe technology and they will, almost certainly, require magnetic stripes to be incorporated on smart cards during a phase-over period.

Applications for the magnetic stripe card in the financial and access areas are well known but new applications, in areas such as vending, are fast emerging.

INTEGRATED CIRCUIT (IC) MEMORY CARDS

Integrated circuit memory cards are mass storage devices. They generally contain much more memory than a smart card, although some that have been designed for specific applications, such as telephone prepaid decrementing cards, have memories of a comparable size to those of smart cards. Unlike smart cards, they have no intelligence in the form of a microprocessor, although they may contain a small amount of dedicated logic for carrying out very simple functions. They are generally available in a package the same size as a credit card but often much thicker – typically, 3mm. Other packages are available and Datakey Inc., for instance, produces its cards in a key format as well as a dog-tag format.

Cards are available in RAM, EEPROM, one-time programmable memory (see Fig. 5.3) and masked ROM memory. Memory capacities are generally very high and it is now possible to carry in your pocket, IC memory cards containing 32kbytes, 512kbytes and 2Mbytes of memory.

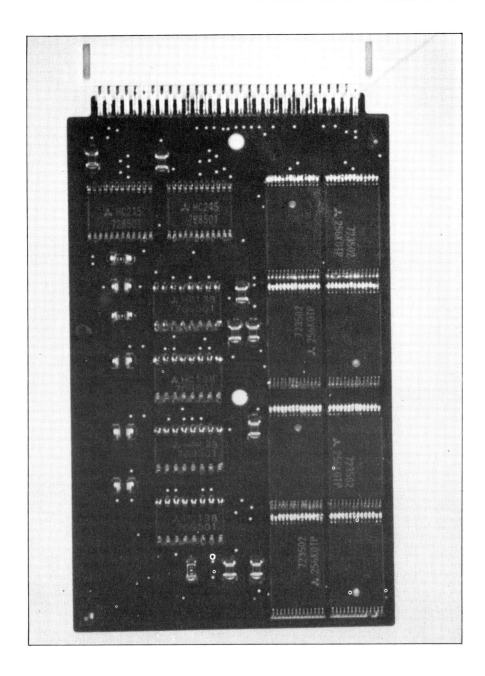

Fig. 5.3. The electronics inside a memory card. (Photograph courtesy of Mitsubishi)

IC memory cards are designed to contain a number of memory chips on a printed circuit board inside the card. Hence, they are generally more expensive than smart cards, because of the number of chips they contain. However, this is not necessarily restrictive as the applications for which they are intended are not usually as price sensitive as some of the large volume applications at which smart cards are targeted.

Information is usually transferred to and from the cards via metal pins or metallic contacts on one of the edges of the card when it is plugged into a connector. The card edge connector often features a protective shutter, which retracts upon card insertion, and there are usually guides to prevent incorrect insertion. The large capacity memory cards dictate that a large number of contacts on the edge of the card are required, particularly as these cards often have 16-bit address and 16-bit data widths. Sixty contacts are not untypical. An IC memory card without contacts is also now available. It is called 'Thrucard' and uses a magnetic coupling method for data transfer.

In the case of the 'memory key', produced by Datakey, the key has to be inserted into a device, known as a Keyceptacle, in order for data to be written to and read from the card's memory (see Fig. 5.4). The contacts coming from the memory within the key are very short for protection. When inserted in the Keyceptacle and rotated 90 degrees, they come into contact with leads on a printed circuit board within the Keyceptacle. Data can then be transferred from or to the key through the Keyceptacle which has been designed to allow it to interface easily with a host system.

The cards, which contain RAM, have lithium button-type batteries for memory retention when power is not being applied to the card's memory. The life of the battery is dependent upon various factors including memory capacity and temperature, but the battery, typically, lasts for five years. The battery can be replaced, without loss of the card's memory contents. Cards are also available which have nickel-cadmium rechargeable batteries. Applications for IC memory cards include software storage, data recording and video/image memory.

OPTICAL MEMORY CARDS – DREXLER LASERCARD

The Drexler LaserCard is the most prominent of the commercially available optical memory cards. It was introduced by Jerome Drexler and was introduced to the market in 1981. Like IC memory cards, the optical card is passive and does not contain a processor. The most

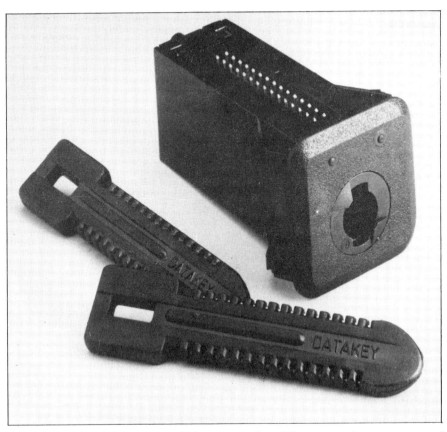

Fig. 5.4. Datakey key and Keyceptacle. (Photograph courtesy of Datakey Inc.)

striking feature of the LaserCard is its 2Mbyte memory capacity – this is equivalent to about 800 pages of text or 60 pages of graphics.

The LaserCard, detailed in Fig. 5.5, consists of two outer layers of polycarbonate plastic between which is sandwiched a strip of Drexon recording medium. The card is coated with a scratch-resistant layer on its optical surface because it is important that, in normal use, the surface does not become so scratched that the card cannot be read. The recording medium consists of a layer of suspended silver particles backed by a non-reflective layer. Recording is carried out using a photolithographic process during which a high-powered laser burns holes in the reflective surface. These holes are equivalent to digital characters when the data is read. The reader employs a lower-powered laser which picks out the non-reflective areas exposed during the recording process.

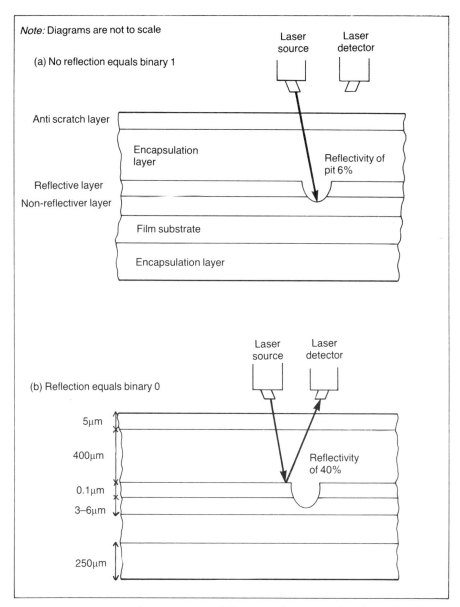

Fig. 5.5. Principle of operation of the Drexler LaserCard

The memory capacity varies according to which type of memory is used. If it is read only the card can hold up to 4Mbytes of information. In this case the recording would be done during the manufacturing process. However, the cards are more likely to be used where they need to be written to as well as read by the end user.

Information on the LaserCard cannot be erased and that means that, once a part of the memory has been written to, that area cannot be used again for new data. The procedure for updating information involves writing the new information on the next available line. Both lines are then cross-referenced so that the reader knows where to look for the rest of the information. This system provides a satisfactory alternative to erasing and rewriting information, given the size of the card's memory. Also, in many applications, it is an advantage to be able to see a complete history of the card's life.

The Drexler Corporation manufactures the cards and has also recently licensed their manufacture to Canon of Japan. The related equipment for reading the cards is manufactured under licence by more than 20 different companies around the world including Canon, Matsushita, Honeywell and Wang. In the early stages it proved difficult to produce reliable and competitively priced (at around $600) readers for LaserCards but, by 1986, some manufacturers had succeeded.

Applications for the optical memory card are in areas where large amounts of memory are required. The card is particularly suitable for medical records as it has the capacity to hold graphical information as well as text. Also, in the field of desk-top publishing, the optical card could be used to distribute 'paperless' publications: paper is a bulky and expensive way of distributing information. An optical storage medium not only has the advantage of being easy to distribute, it can also be used to download information on to the user's computer for further processing and updating. Record keeping is another application where the optical memory card's use is particularly appropriate.

TAGS

A tag could be defined as a contactless memory card. Like the contactless smart card it works without coming into contact with the reader. It also contains memory, although much less than is found in memory cards. Unlike the smart card it does not, generally, contain intelligence in the form of a microprocessor and the nature of the electronics within it prevents it from being made into an ISO card. As its name implies, the applications to which a tag is put are normally related to tracking and identification – for example, tracking of manufactured articles on a production line or allowing personnel access to a secure area. Coded tags come in a range of different packages to suit specific applications (see Fig. 5.6).

The transmission method most frequently used is radio frequency and the complete system is often referred to as radio frequency identification (RF/ID). In the simplest RF/ID systems, the object to be identified carries a transmitter which is activated only when a signal of a certain frequency is received. It then sends its identification in response. The transmitter/receiver pair, or *transceiver*, together with the memory, attached to the object are referred to by manufacturers as the tag (sometimes the transponder).

The device carrying out the interrogation is referred to as a *scanner* or *interrogator*. The most common term for the complete subsystem, including the intelligence to interpret the information, is *reader*. Scanners and readers come in a variety of forms including hand-held wands, loops or arrays, mounted in walls or buried in roadways and floors, and a variety of boxes and panels.

The simplest RF/ID system is one in which the reader sends a specific frequency without any form of data transfer. The tag, upon receipt of

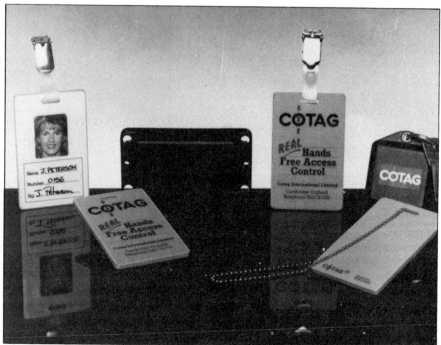

Fig. 5.6. Coded tags come in a range of different packages to suit specific applications (Photograph courtesy of Cotag)

this signal, responds on a different frequency. This secondary frequency is recognised by the reader as the appropriate response from a tag in its system. Of course, if another device happened to radiate that frequency, the reader might be fooled into believing that a tag was present and would respond accordingly.

Another potential problem is that two or more tags could be present within the operating range of the reader. The reader could only report that something that appeared to be a tag was present. Even if the tags were widely spaced, so that only one was within operating range at a time, the system would not be able to differentiate between them. These problems can be overcome by making the tag respond with a unique identification code.

All tag systems have one or more antennae – the conductive elements which radiate and/or receive energy in the radio frequency spectrum. They are fabricated in a variety of ways, influenced by requirements such as cost, range, directionality, size or environment. They may be coils of wire – with or without ferrite cores – metal foil plates or a variety of patterns rendered in copper on a printed circuit board.

The antennae, transmitter and receiver electronics may be integrated in a single package to form the scanner or may be combined with additional digital electronics, including a microprocessor, to form the reader. The digital electronics perform the actual reading function, looking at the received bit patterns in order to extract and separate the information from the format definition and error management bits. The read electronics may also include an interface to an integral display and/or provide a parallel or serial communications interface to a host computer or industrial controller.

All of these elements, including the scanner, may be packaged together, or the read electronics may be packaged separately. If this complete set of electronics is able to change the contents of tags while they remain attached to their objects, it is called a reader/writer.

Readers are also built as battery-powered portable units or they may incorporate a display or printer for visually presenting tag data. Some include computer interfaces and non-volatile memory for temporary storage of data from multiple tags, which is to be uploaded to a computer at a later time.

RF/ID products may be differentiated and classified in a variety of ways. One of these is by the frequencies used:

● *Low-frequency* products use frequencies below 500kHz. Just as AM radio has the advantage of not being line-of-sight, low-frequency

RF/ID is also unaffected by non-conductive obstructions. Transmissions pass through wood, plastic, ceramic, plaster, glass, grease, and even, concrete.

- *Medium frequency* is usually the range from 1.7MHz to 28MHz. New products using this band may start to appear within the next year or two. The higher data rates will be beneficial when tags with larger memory capacities are being used and there is more data to be transferred. Medium-frequency tags can operate over larger ranges than their lower frequency counterparts.

- *High-frequency* products currently use frequencies ranging from 908MHz to 5.8GHz. The most significant advantage that high-frequency products enjoy is range. High-frequency signals can be focused in a beam. When equivalent energy is directed as a beam it has greater range than energy that is propagated omni-directionally. This allows operation at ranges of up to 150ft. with active tags, and 30 - 40 ft. with passive tags. The reflection of the signal from an object other than the tag is a potential source of difficulty in high-frequency systems.

RF/ID products can also be divided into two major categories according to the power source of the tag. Tags that are internally powered are called active and, typically, incorporate batteries. Passive tags contain no internal power source. They, typically, derive their power from the signal radiated by the reader.

In order to be identifiers of specific objects tags must, at some point, have an identity and other data entered into them. This programming can be done in three different ways:

- *Factory programming* – when the programming occurs as part of the manufacturing process. Factory programming can be accomplished by, for instance, passing a large current through conductive links, thereby removing some links, similar to deliberately blowing fuses. It can also be done electronically, by storing data in various forms of ROM and RAM.

- *Field programming*. Programming may occur after the tags have been shipped from the manufacturer to intermediate customers or end users, or in some cases to the manufacturer's distribution locations. This usually occurs before the tag is installed on the object to be identified. Field programming may be achieved electrically (through contacts left accessible in the final level of packaging) or by RF coupling with the programming device, usually while in close proximity to it. This approach allows data relevant to the specific application to be introduced into the tag at any time. In some cases, a portion of the device is reserved for factory programming. This might include a unique tag serial number, for example.

- *In-use programming*. Many applications require that new data or revisions to data already in the tag be entered into the tag while it remains attached to its object. The ability to read from and write data to the tag while attached to its object is called in-use programming. The tags are called read/write (R/W) tags.

Organising tags by capacity is a useful way to indicate the type or classes of applications that various products would typically address. Capacities of tags are commonly described in four levels where increasing capacity represents an increase in cost. The levels are:

- *Level I.* Presence-sensing tags provide one bit of data capacity.They are most commonly used in electronic article-surveillance applications to prevent the theft of retail goods from stores. Such tags, costing pennies or less, can be 'turned off' or disabled before leaving the store while still attached to the merchandise. Similar tags are also used in industrial environments in which hazards exist for the workers. Tags on the workers are sensed by readers located near the hazard and cause either a warning to be sounded or a shut down of the equipment which constitutes the hazard. Most of these tags are factory programmed but field programming is becoming more popular.
- *Level II.* Identification tags typically provide from 8 to 128 bits of memory as a means of differentiating between members of a population of people or items having some attributes in common. In some cases the tags contain unique codes while in other cases they are not duplicated within a specific population. Relevant data regarding the attributes of the object are stored in a database, which is accessed by the individual identification codes.
- *Level III.* Transaction/routing tags containing from 48 to 512 bits of memory are an extension of Level II to include sufficient capacity to carry data beyond simple identity. Often this additional capacity is used to store milestones or events in a transaction or series of transactions. It may also be used to store the intended routing or processing of the tag's object and can include the record of progress. Levels II and III tags are in-use programmable or read/write tags.
- *Level IV.* Portable database tags containing from 256 bits to more than 128kbytes are currently being used. Obviously these can hold substantial amounts of alphanumeric text.

A few of the applications where tags can be used have already been mentioned briefly. However, tags are suitable for use in a wide variety of applications and are currently being used in areas as diverse as routing and tracking, container identification, facility access by personnel, vehicle access tolls, automatic animal feeding and rail carriage identification.

INTELLIGENT TOKENS – NPL TOKEN

The National Physical Laboratory (NPL) in Britain has been working for some time on the development of a token, called Talisman, which can provide far greater security than is possible through the use of a PIN alone. The NPL has used the RSA public key encryption system (described fully in Chapter 7), implemented on a Texas Instruments microprocessor within the token, to provide highly secure digital signatures.

The aim is to enable the token to sign messages electronically using a unique secret key which is never revealed to the terminal. The terminal must be equipped with RSA capability in the same way as the token so that it can carry out procedures to check the generated digital signatures. The terminal also needs to have the token's public key in order to verify the messages. So far smart cards have not been able to use this system of encryption because it requires more processing power, memory and speed than is currently available in a smart card. The NPL token, however, can carry out a full RSA transformation in 1.5 seconds.

The token uses two processors – a digital signal processor and an 8-bit microcomputer – which are arranged in two modules (see Fig. 5.7). The RSA module incorporates the digital signal processor and its associated ROM and RAM memory storage. The control module contains the microcomputer, ROM and RAM storage, time of day clock, input/output interface, display and keypad. The two modules communicate via a bus buffer. The token receives and sends messages via a 3-wire serial interface and would normally communicate with a terminal which would provide the power. The token can also be used with a second processor board added to it, with an IBM PC-compatible computer. A total of 11 chips are used in the MK2 token shown in the figure.

The identification procedure begins with the token being presented to the terminal. The token then identifies itself to the terminal, which responds by sending out a challenge in the form of a random number. When the token receives the challenge it asks the cardholder to enter

Fig. 5.7. The prototype NPL Talisman token MK2 (Crown Copyright)

his PIN via the token's keypad. The PIN is then compared to the number stored in memory. If the PIN is correct the token generates a digital signature on the challenge and returns the signed challenge to the terminal.

In the mean time, the terminal has obtained the token's public key, either from a register or from the token itself. The public key allows the terminal to check the signature on the challenge. If the terminal is satisfied that the signature on the challenge is valid it has proved also that the token is valid and that the person using it knows the correct PIN. If the token receives the wrong PIN on the first attempt it will ask the cardholder to enter the number again. After a third unsuccessful attempt the token is programmed to stop requesting the PIN and overwrite the store containing the secret key which is used to generate the digital signature. This prevents someone systematically searching for the correct PIN and also disables the token completely. Special control procedures are needed to restore the token before it can be used again.

The token's ability to sign messages can be extended to financial transactions. In this case the identification procedure is as before. The transaction message shown by the terminal is passed to the token for checking and shown on the token's LCD display. The user indicates

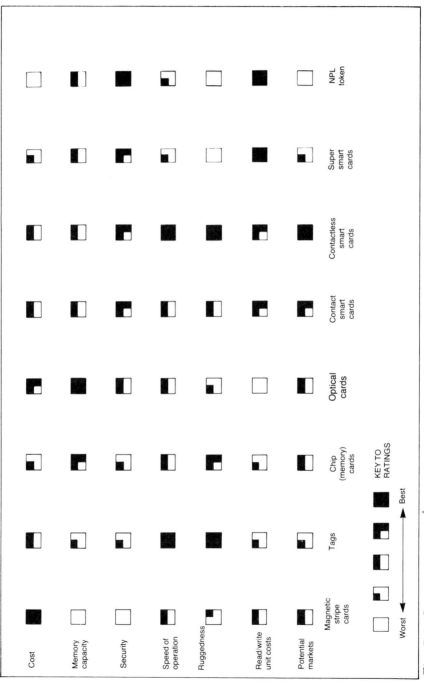

Fig. 5.8. Comparison of smart cards and related devices

his acceptance via the keypad and the token adds the date and time, signs the message and returns it to the terminal. The addition of the date and time to the message is an extra precaution against tampering.

The possible applications for the NPL intelligent token are in the same areas as for smart cards generally. It is not, however, anticipated that attempts will be made to make the token conform to ISO standards for financial transaction cards. The present prototype is the size of a small book but it is expected that the final version will be the size of a small pocket calculator. It is likely that the token will always be more expensive to produce than the smart card and it is probable, therefore, that its main areas of application will be where the security requirement outweighs cost considerations.

COMPARISON

As there is now such a variety of smart cards and related devices on the market it is important to be able to compare their characteristics when deciding on the suitability of a particular device for a particular application. Therefore, in Fig. 5.8 an attempt is made to summarise the relative advantages and disadvantages of the various characteristics of smart cards and other related devices.

6

MANUFACTURE, PERSONALISATION AND ISSUE

THERE ARE eight major stages involved in the manufacture, personalisation and issue of smart cards. They are shown in Fig. 6.1 and are as follows:

- *Design*. Designing the card to a written specification which meets market requirements, such as cost, satisfies a multiplicity of different applications, will operate in a range of environments and survive under normal wear and tear conditions for a specified period of time. The design should accommodate the possibility of scaling up to very large volume manufacture. Unlike the operations that follow, design is not a process that is repeated except when a new generation of card is to be produced.

Fig. 6.1. The stages involved in manufacturing a smart card

- *Chip fabrication*. Manufacture of the smart card chip or chips.
- *Embedding software in permanent memory*. Storage of fundamental instructions required for all applications, such as sending data to the reader, are stored in the card's permanent memory.
- *Micromodule manufacture*. Production of a circuit board (rigid or flexible) and the mounting of the chip or chips on the board prior to incorporation of the module in the card.
- *Embedding the micromodule in a card*. The use of traditional card lamination techniques or other techniques to produce a non-active card including the embedding of the micromodule in the card.
- *Application program development*. Writing of the application software to a specification.
- *Activation*. Incorporation of the application software in the card, together with security keys if they are required.
- *Personalisation and issue*. Storage, in the card, of personal identification data relating to the ultimate cardholder and the issue of the card to the intended owner, such that no mismatch occurs with personal data stored in the card.

DESIGN

A number of factors need to be taken into consideration when designing the card.

The manufacturing process

The chips in the card may have to withstand heat and pressure during the manufacturing process and when a magnetic stripe and signature panel are added. The embossing process can also damage the chips.

Environment and use

In normal use the chips can be vulnerable to wear and tear and to their environment. To counteract this, the area of the chip should be as small as possible. A chip with a large area will suffer more physical stress when the card is bent and twisted. It must be able to withstand the ordinary wear and tear of life, like being carried in a back pocket and being sat upon, or being trodden on. One problem has been encountered with some contact smart cards when mailing them through the British Post Office network, though such problems have not been reported from other countries. It appears that rollers used in the sorting office are liable to damage the chip unless it is adequately protected.

The smart card will often need to function in an electronically noisy situation created by magnetic or electromagnetic fields from such sources as electrical and radio equipment. For example, when a card is inserted into an automatic dispensing machine, such as a petrol pump, the card's own signals must be able to compete with those of the pump.

Cards must be able to withstand electrostatic charges because in certain environments there may be a large static electricity build-up which may distort or destroy normal chip operation. The action may, in fact, be sporadic and inconsistent. A dry room with thick rugs in a warm environment might be sufficient to generate damaging levels of electrostatic charge.

The card must be able to withstand wide variations in temperature – if it is left on a car dashboard, for instance, it can reach a high temperature. If it is used for scraping ice off a windscreen, it could go to the other extreme of temperature. If it is then dropped on a road which has been treated with salt, the card can suffer the corrosive effects of brine. It must be capable of working in hot, humid climates such as Singapore and cold climates such as Finland.

The functioning of the card must not be impaired if liquids, such as coffee or petrol, are spilt on it – in dirty environments a contactless smart card may be the answer.

The chip must not be damaged, or its memory erased, if the card passes through an X-ray machine at an airport.

Standards

Existing equipment, such as ATMs, are not going to be discarded overnight. A smart card must, therefore, be capable of being used in the current generation of machines as well as in smart card based equipment. Eventually there will be a migration from the old to the new but, in the mean time, the two types of technology must coexist. This means that the card must have the same dimensions, incorporate a magnetic stripe and be embossable: in fact, meet the international standards laid down for magnetic stripe cards.

This is primarily true for smart cards used in financial applications. It is not necessarily true in new applications for cards, such as medical applications, where there is not an existing card base and standards have not yet been established. However, whatever standards are established, whether or not they follow the financial transaction card standards, they must be adhered to because of the international nature of the cards.

It is no mean feat to create a smart card that meets the existing ISO standards on the thickness dimension (0.76mm ± 10%), flexing, and survival over a wide range of temperatures and humidity, as well as having the capability to be embossed and to incorporate a magnetic stripe.

Application range

The application for which the card is intended determines the amount of memory it will need. For use as a telephone card, for instance, only a small memory is required. If the card is used as a distribution medium for computer programs, on the other hand, a large memory capacity is needed. The proportion of non-programmable memory (ROM) and reprogrammable memory (e.g. EEPROM) is also a function of the applications in which the card is to be used.

Cost

Less than £5 per card is seen as the large volume viable selling price for a general-purpose, multi-function smart card. For a dedicated application requiring a lot less memory, such as for telephone call payments, the card needs to cost much less than £5.

The cost of the card is determined by:

- The type of card – contact, contactless or super smart. The fewer the parts required to make up the card the less it costs to manufacture.
- Memory capacity. More memory means higher cost.
- The type of memory used. EEPROM is more costly than EPROM because, capacity for capacity, it has more chip area.
- Material costs.
- The number manufactured. Large volume manufacture results in economy of scale.
- The number of production processes.
- The degree of automation in the production line. Manual production processes create higher costs.

Other considerations

As an electrical device, the chip will need to be able to dissipate the heat it generates when power is applied. The amount of power applied, and its duration, will determine the heat generated. Heat generated is also a function of the chip technology, capacity and use. For example, a chip with dense content will experience heavy heat build-up during its program loading and personalisation process.

The card surface temperature should not be allowed to exceed 50°C, at which level some card materials start to soften. Any higher temperature could distort the card and, if the surface becomes too warm, there is a possibility that the chips may pop out of the surface. To counteract this danger it may be necessary to use a heat dissipation element, such as a thermally conductive network around the chip, to reduce thermal gradients within the card, eliminate hot spots and allow the entire card surface to radiate any heat.

The chip must not malfunction in the electromagnetic field that is used to write information to and read from the magnetic stripe that may be incorporated on the card. All the card's sealed surfaces must remain unbroken throughout its life and in particular the card layers must not peel apart.

CHIP FABRICATION

The material from which chips are made is silicon. Selective processing can turn the silicon into two types – p-type and n-type – in which they function as metal oxide semiconductors (MOS). Combined in various different ways they form the circuit elements of the chip – transistors, resistors, diodes and small capacitors. When the silicon used is mainly p-type, the technology is referred to as PMOS; when it is mainly n-type, it is known as NMOS. If a combination of both types of silicon is used the technology is called CMOS, or complementary MOS. The characteristics of both PMOS and NMOS allow elements to be densely packed on a chip. The chips are also inexpensive to produce and are fast in operation.

The disadvantage of these technologies is that they can be sensitive to extraneous electrical signals (noise) from other devices and this could be a problem in many smart card applications. CMOS technology is the least sensitive to electrical noise and has the advantage of drawing far less power. It therefore creates less heat in operation, making it far more suitable for use in smart cards. The main stages of chip manufacture are as follows:

- Creation of an ingot of pure silicon.
- Preparation of thin circular slices of this silicon crystal, called *wafers*.

- The surface characteristics of the wafer are altered to give the required semiconductor and electrical properties, such as resistance. The end result is a wafer comprising several hundred chips.
- Individual chips are tested to locate good and bad devices.
- Wafers are sometimes back lapped to reduce thickness, and are diced – sawn or scribed to separate individual chips.

Creation of an ingot of pure silicon

The raw silicon is first reduced from its oxide, using a series of chemical steps, until it reaches a state of almost 100% purity. A quantity of pure silicon is then brought to its melting point (1,420°C) in an atmosphere of inert gas. Impurities, known as dopants, are then added to the silicon to produce a specific type of conductivity, i.e. p-type or n-type.

A single perfect silicon crystal, known as a seed, is then inserted into the melted silicon and slowly turned and pulled as it is withdrawn. In this way single crystals, 2in. - 6in. in diameter and several feet long, can be grown from the original seed.

Preparation of wafers

When the crystal has cooled the surface is ground to produce a cylinder of a standard diameter, usually 5in. (125mm). The cylinder is sliced into circular discs (see Fig.6.2) called wafers, of about 0.02in. (0.5mm) thickness using a thin, high speed diamond saw. Finally, the wafer is polished on one side and smoothed on the other. The smooth side must not be scratched or have any defects or chemical impurities.

Wafer fabrication

A film of silicon dioxide is formed on the surface of the wafer by heating it in an atmosphere of oxygen or steam. The silicon dioxide layer is hard, adheres well and acts as an excellent insulator. The thickness of the oxide layer can be varied by controlling the temperature and the length of time the wafer is exposed to the oxygen or steam.

The wafers are processed in bulk inside a furnace. A fine control is kept on the temperature and atmosphere inside the furnace, the rate of insertion and withdrawal and the length of time the wafers spend in the furnace.

Layers are grown on the wafer, in particular patterns, to produce the required properties of an individual circuit. The patterns are transferred to each wafer by a process of photo-engraving known as

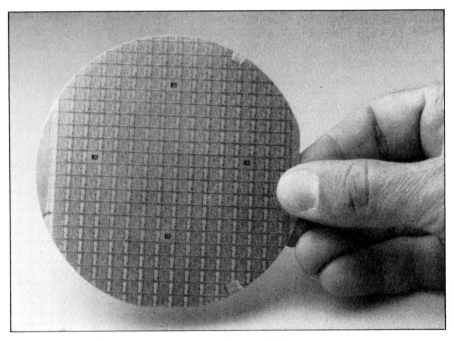

Fig. 6.2. A wafer containing a number of chips

photolithography. A series of photo masks, together with photo-sensitive emulsions, are used to produce different individual patterns on the wafer so that a sandwich is built up.

The photolithography process is carried out in stages. First, the silicon wafer, with an oxide layer, is covered with photoresist. This is applied in a solvent and, as the solvent evaporates, the hard photo-resist remains on the surface. The photoresist is heated afterwards to ensure that it is completely dry and has adhered to the oxide surface. The wafer is then exposed to ultraviolet light through a mask, which transfers the pattern to the surface. The areas which have been exposed are frozen or fixed.

The wafer is then washed and chemicals are used to remove the areas of photoresist which have not been exposed. This reveals the areas of silicon dioxide underneath. The silicon and polymerised photoresist which have been exposed are not affected and remain on the wafer.

The silicon diode revealed when the photoresist has been removed is removed by using an ethant, leaving a pattern of bare silicon unprotected. The remaining photoresist is then removed and the wafer is placed in a furnace containing a doped atmosphere. The dopants diffuse into the silicon where the silicon dioxide has been removed, and the boundaries between the various doped zones form the semiconductor junctions. More layers are built up in the same way. The wafers will be in the furnace several times during processing and the total time spent in the furnace is important in determining the result of the process.

The upper layers of the wafer are made up of thin conductive films. One of these is the interconnect layer. This is often aluminium or polysilicon and it performs the same function as the copper layer on a printed circuit board, connecting the individual circuits together. The layer of aluminium is deposited by evaporation or chemical vapour deposition and the pattern is again defined by usings masks and photoresist.

Layers of protective material are finally deposited on the wafer. Glass, doped with phosphorus, and silicon nitride are used to prevent damage from scratching and moisture ingress. The bonding pads, to which the external connections will be made, are left uncovered.

Testing

In the final stage of processing each individual chip on the wafer is tested. This is known as probe testing and is carried out under the control of a computer containing the test program. Any defective chips are marked by an ink spot and later discarded. The testing of an individual chip takes only a couple of seconds and the probe moves on to the next chip automatically.

Back lapping and wafer scribing

It may be necessary at this stage to reduce the thickness of the chips – if a final card thickness within ISO standards is to be achieved. This is carried out by a process known as back lapping. The side of the wafer that has not had the chip pattern built up on it is ground down using an abrasive powder until it is of the correct thickness. Only when the chips have reached the designated thickness are they diced into individual chips.

The chips can be diced or separated by simply scribing the wafer between the chips and breaking along the scribe lines. A typical scribe could be a laser or a diamond. It is usual to transport chips in a complete wafer, so waxed paper is applied to the back of the wafer to make the chips stay together immediately after dicing. The good chips are separated later for use in the cards.

EMBEDDING THE SOFTWARE IN ROM

For the chip to function it must have software embedded in the ROM. As discussed previously, this can be either a general-purpose operating system written by the card manufacturer or one of a number of defined options suitable for different types of applications (as for the Bull CP8 card). Alternatively it can be software for a specific customer's application requiring large numbers of cards.

The process of embedding the software in the ROM is known as masking or customising the ROM. During manufacture, the mask layers are produced as described previously but a layer, known as the programmable layer, is left uncustomised. It is this layer that is used to interconnect certain circuit elements and, hence, to store the card manufacturer's operating system, general program options or the card issuer's application program. The sequence of operations in masking the ROM, depicted in Fig. 6.3, is as follows:

- The customer – card manufacturer or card issuer – produces the software program he wishes to be stored in ROM.
- The program is sent to the chip manufacturer in the form of an EPROM or floppy disk.
- The chip manufacturer produces a process pattern generation (PG) tape which defines the interconnections for the programmable layers and a new EPROM containing the program. The PG tape is used to produce the masked ROM.
- The new EPROM is sent to the customer for checking. When the customer has checked that the EPROM is correct, the chip manufacturer produces the customised ROM chip in a standard dual-in-line ceramic package which is delivered to the customer. The device is evaluated by the customer to ensure that the ROM is correctly encoded. Chips that are delivered at this stage do not necessarily meet the full specification with regard to operating temperature range and so on.
- When the customer approves the design, the chip manufacturer makes prototype samples which are guaranteed to meet the specification fully. The fully engineered samples are delivered to the customer for evaluation.
- When the customer is satisfied that the samples function properly, mass production of the chips can begin.

These nine processes can take between 18 and 28 weeks, depending on whether or not they are carried out in parallel.

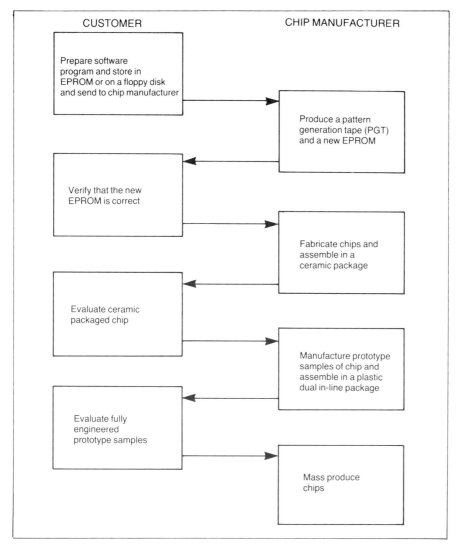

Fig. 6.3. Software embedding cycle for masked ROM

MICROMODULE MANUFACTURE

The next stage in the production of a smart card is to mount the chip or chips on a printed circuit board. This is necessary for both contact and contactless types of smart cards. The board can be either rigid or flexible and is often referred to as the substrate.

Producing the substrate

The substrate consists of a layer of insulating material, such as polyimide or epoxy glass, on which there are conducting tracks which connect the chip to contact pads on the surface of the card or a loop aerial – and in a multi-chip card, to other chips. The substrate is produced by taking the insulating layer with a complete covering of copper, coating it with photoresist and exposing it to ultraviolet light through a mask consisting of the pattern of the conducting tracks. The exposed areas of resist are then chemically washed away to reveal the unwanted areas of copper. The unwanted copper is then etched off. The remaining photoresist is removed with another chemical. The result is a thin layer of insulating material carrying copper conducting tracks.

Connecting the chip to the substrate

The chip can be connected to the substrate using one of several methods: wire bonding, tape automated bonding (TAB) or 'flip chip'.

Wire bonding. This is the most commonly-used method in the chip industry of connecting pads (outer connections of the chip) to the leads of the package in which the chip is to be encapsulated. In the case of the smart card, the method involves connecting a thin 25μm gold or aluminium wire from each individual pad to the correct conducting track of the substrate, as in Fig. 6.4.

Tape automated bonding. Known as TAB, this much newer method has advantages and disadvantages over wire bonding. When TAB is used the chips are mounted on a continuous tape of film similar to photographic film. The tape is usually made up of polyimide and copper foil with an adhesive layer to join them together (see Fig. 6.5). Before the copper is glued to the tape, square holes, 0.2mm-1mm larger than the chip, are punched into the polyimide. Beam leads are then made on the copper foil using a process of photoresist, masking and etching. The chips cannot be mounted on the tape until the connecting pads are 'bumped'. This is a process whereby metallisation layers are grown on the chip's bonding pads to raise them above the surface of the rest of the chip. The bonding of the bumped chip to the tape is known as inner lead bonding. This is a temperature pressure process which is carried out using a device known as a thermode.

  The chips are punched out along the perimeter of the square in the polyimide, leaving single chips with beam leads which may be

Fig. 6.4. A chip wire bonded to a substrate for insertion into a contact card (Photograph courtesy of Schlumberger)

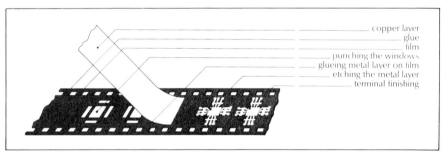

copper layer
glue
film
punching the windows
glueing metal layer on film
etching the metal layer
terminal finishing

Fig. 6.5. Construction of continuous film used in TAB. (Diagram courtesy of EM Microelectronic-Marin SA)

supported by polyimide support rings coming from their pads. They are then positioned automatically and the ends of the leads are bonded to the copper tracks of the substrate, typically by reflow soldering. This process is known as outer lead bonding.

The TAB process depicted in Fig. 6.6 has some advantages over wire bonding. For instance, connections are flatter and this makes it easier

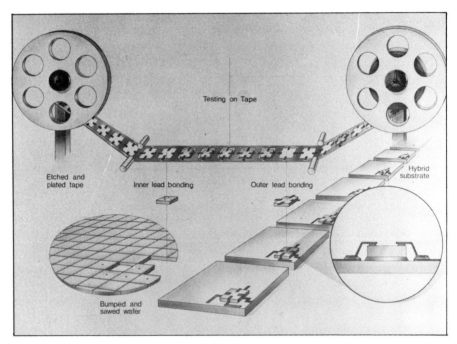

Fig. 6.6. The TAB process (Diagram courtesy of Farco SA)

to encapsulate them in cards which are only 0.76mm thick. The bonds are stronger and less likely to be broken when a card is flexed, and all leads can be bonded at the same time, unlike wire bonding where each lead has to be bonded separately. It is also easier to test the chips immediately before they are put into the card, while they are mounted on a continuous tape. Weighed against these advantages is the need for an extra processing stage to produce bumps on the chips.

Flip chip. This is an earlier technique which involves bumping the input/output (IO) pads of the chip with solder bumps. The chip is then inverted and placed, bumpside down, on the copper wiring 'footprint' on the substrate. The temperature is raised until the solder bumps reflow and form a joint between the chip and the substrate.

Disadvantages of this technique include poor inspectability of the joint and bumping the chip. The process is, however, cheap and simple. A comparison of the connection methods is given in Fig. 6.7.

Glob topping

The material traditionally used in the manufacture of cards is PVC.

Tab	Wire bond	Flip chip
Chip bumping required	No chip bumping	Chip bumping required
Simultaneous bonds to chip	Sequential single bonds to chip	Simultaneous bonds to chip
Low bond profile	High bond profile	Very low bond profile
Pre-test on tape possible immediately prior to assembly	No pre-test immediately prior to assembly	No pre-test immediately prior to assembly
Special bonding tools required	General-purpose bonding tools can be used	Special assembly equipment required
More suited to flow-line automation	Less suited to flow-line automation	Reasonably suited to flow line automation
Relatively new technique	Well-proven technique	Rarely applied technique

Fig. 6.7. Comparison of TAB, wire bond and flip chip technologies

This can, however, produce hydrochloric acid when it degrades in damp conditions. Alternative materials can contain other ionic matter and the chips need to be protected from possible corrosion and contamination from such sources. A process known as glob topping is used for this purpose. This consists of coating the chips with a layer of epoxy, or some other inert protective material, before they are mounted in the card.

EMBEDDING THE MICROMODULE

There are three basic methods of producing the finished card incorporating the micromodule:

- By laminating a PVC layer or layers and transparent top and bottom covers (known as coverlays) to form a card, boring out a hole in this card and gluing the micromodule into the hole. This method is only applicable to contact cards.
- By laminating the micromodule in the middle of a 'sandwich' comprising PVC layers and transparent top and bottom covers.
- By injection moulding.

Lamination and bored hole

The most widely used method of laminating cards involves joining together four different layers: the top graphics layer, the top coverlay, the bottom graphics layer and the bottom coverlay. The graphics layers are printed with the designs for the front and back of the card. The coverlays are the transparent layers that protect the graphics layers. The four layers are sandwiched together and joined by a lamination process involving heat and pressure. If a magnetic stripe is required it generally forms part of the sandwich.

The cards are usually laminated in sheets in a matrix of eight by eight cards. In some of the newer card production plants, cards are produced on a flow line. This allows the process to be more automated and reduces manning levels. The addition of holograms and signature panels is usually carried out using a heat and pressure process known as hot stamping.

Contact cards are usually produced by inserting the micromodule into a hole in the card. The advantage of adding the micromodule at this stage is that it cannot be damaged by the heat and pressure that is applied during the lamination process. The circular, blind hole for the micromodule is bored from one side of the card through most of its thickness. The micromodule, often moulded into a protective pellet with the eight gold plated contacts exposed on its surface, is glued into the hole and sealed so that the contacts are accessible on the outer surface of the card (see Fig. 6.8).

Embedding the micromodule in a laminated sandwich

This assembly method is usually applied when more complex and larger micromodules are used. A PVC layer, which is an inverse image of the micromodule, is placed on top of the micromodule. That is, wherever there is a component in the micromodule there is a recess in the covering layer. On either side of this central core are placed the graphics layers and coverlays which, in the case of a contact card, must also have holes for the contacts. The complete 'sandwich' is then laminated together to form the card (see Fig 6.9).

Injection moulding

The manufacturing technology used in the production of plastic cards originated from traditional printing techniques, largely because investment had already been made in offset printing machines. It was a natural course to translate established techniques to the printing of PVC sheets when production of plastic cards began. It was still possible to use the same basic technology and machines when magnetic stripes and holograms began to be added and it was assumed that the tried and tested methods would also be able to deal with the

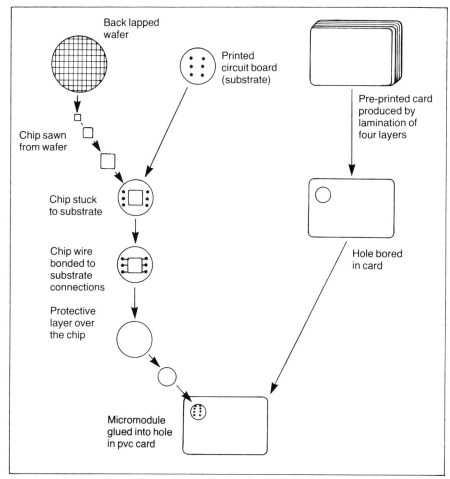

Fig. 6.8. Typical assembly process for contact cards by inserting the micromodule into a hole bored in the card

new requirement to package a chip within a credit card.

One alternative, being adopted by companies such as Gemplus Card International, is injection moulding, which offers the opportunity of putting the plastic around the chip instead of putting the chip inside thè plastic.

Injection moulding is best known in the manufacture of small plastic articles. The usual method is to heat small granules of the plastic until they melt and then inject the liquid into a mould at high temperature and pressure, perhaps 300°C and 2,000lb/in^2. The plastic then sets in the mould as it cools.

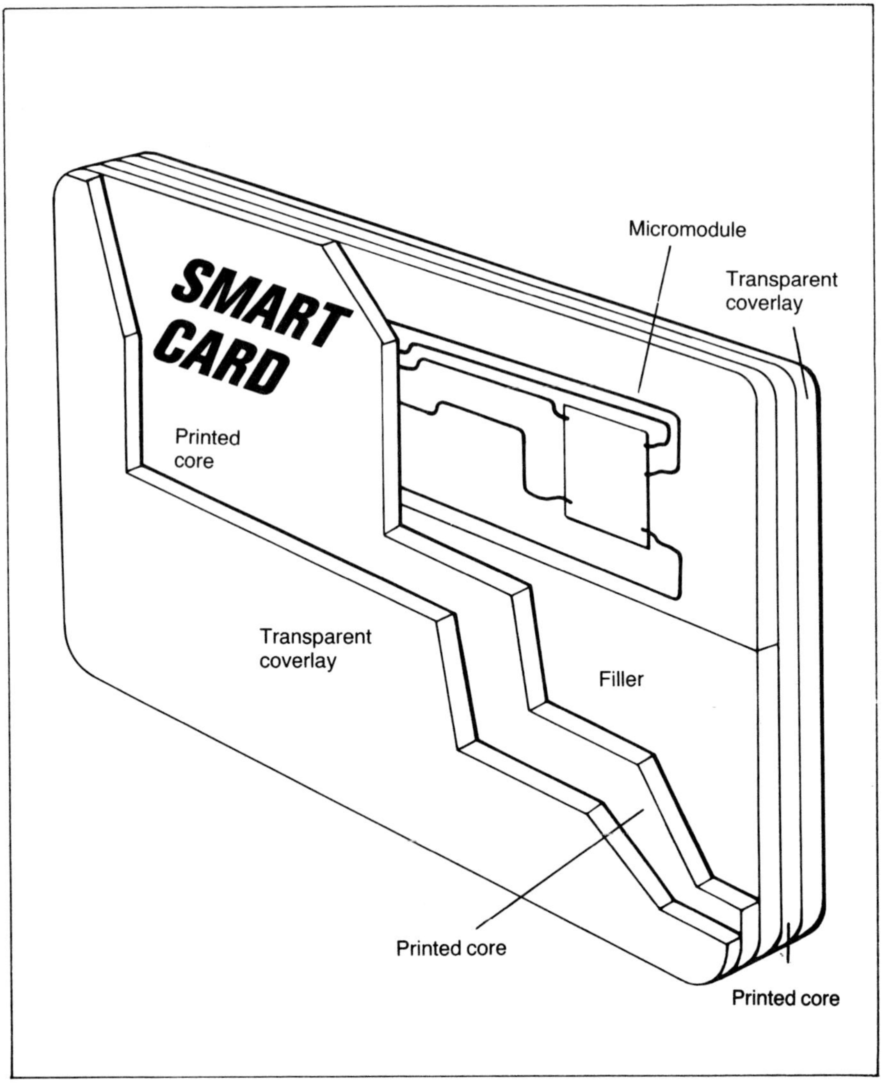

Fig. 6.9. Schematic diagram showing a micromodule which is laminated in a sandwich

The method currently used for the Gemplus contact type card is to mould the card in white with a cavity into which the chip module, complete with contacts, is inserted and glued. The chip is then tested and coded, after which the card is individually printed before final quality assurance and dispatch. Alternatively, printing can be done before the module is inserted.

Cards are moulded four at a time. Granular ABS plastic to an anti-static formulation is automatically moved from the holding bin to a pre-processing storage tank which is controlled to ensure precise temperature and humidity conditions for the plastic. The plastic is transferred to the input chamber of the injection moulding machine and injected, under pressure, into the four-card mould. From the moulding machine the cards are removed by a robot and transferred to a trimming station where they are separated and any excess plastic is removed. The same robot finally moves them to the micromodule assembly station.

Here, the micromodule assembly robot places the cards into fixtures which locate them precisely. The station deposits adhesive in the four cavities simultaneously, picks up four micromodules and inserts them into the cavities. The assembled cards are then loaded into an output fixture where the micromodules are kept under pressure during the initial curing period of the adhesive. At this stage electrical tests and encoding operations can also be carried out.

The white cards can be moved immediately to the printing stage or can undergo further processing to suit customer requirements. Printing is done using compact four-colour offset equipment. Cards are held pneumatically during the four-stage printing and then go through a fixed ultraviolet ink curing stage. Final printing stages allow the card to have personalised printing and a protective anti-static coating added.

Injection moulding machine manufacturer Netstal Maschinen of Switzerland provides equipment for Schlumberger and Gemplus employing an eight-cavity mould supplied by Seropa (see Fig. 6.10). Removal of the cards from the mould is done by a hydraulic robot using vacuum suckers as ejector pins in the mould would damage the cards. The robot works to a six second cycle time.

Netstal is also working on a new process which will produce smart cards in one step. With this technique the chip is mounted directly into the mould, and is moulded into the card. According to Netstal, problems related to the injection temperature, and its effect on the chips, are being overcome.

APPLICATION PROGRAM DEVELOPMENT

A specific application program for the smart card can be developed by either the card manufacturer or the customer. This stage is only applicable to smart cards with application programs that have not

Fig. 6.10. Netsal machine employing four-cavity Seropa mould

already been masked in ROM and which are able to have the program embedded in programmable memory, such as EEPROM.

The first stage in writing the program is to produce the requirements specification for the application and then to write the software to meet the requirements specification. A personal computer is usually used for this. When the software is written it can be tested using an emulator. An emulator is usually made up of a printed circuit board containing both a microprocessor, which is functionally the same as the one to be used in the card, and a memory, which represents the card's memory. The emulator is connected to the computer on which the software is being developed as shown in Fig. 6.11.

The program in the computer is loaded into the emulator which then acts as a smart card communicating with a computer. The emulator allows the program to be stopped at various points so that checks can be made on memory contents and so on, to see if the software is functioning as expected. The emulator also allows data to be written into areas of the memory for test purposes.

The emulator can be used to test the software as it is built up stage by stage until a fully working program has been produced. Other forms of development tools, such as software simulators, are also available for program development.

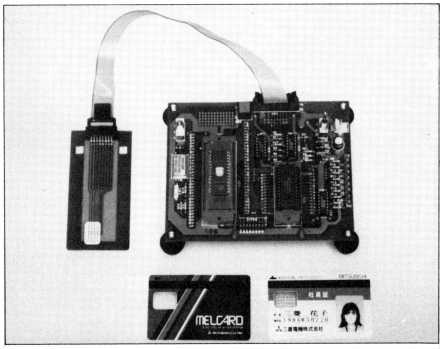

Fig. 6.11. Emulator and other tools for developing the application program. (Photographs courtesy of Mitsubishi)

ACTIVATION

Other features, such as security keys, are integrated into the application program at this stage. The program and keys are loaded via a read/write unit into each card from a computer where they are stored. The cards are then packaged and dispatched to the issuer.

Security is of great importance during the whole manufacturing process. Cards are usually produced in very secure premises and there are procedures to account for all chips and materials used – so that none can be stolen to manufacture fraudulent cards.

PERSONALISATION AND ISSUE

Details, fed into the card at this stage by the issuer, relate to the individual to whom the card will belong. For example, in a financial application they will probably include the person's name, spending limit, and PIN. These details are stored in the various memory zones described in Chapter 3. The open zone, for instance, would contain the name and address. The working zone would probably remain blank and the secret zone would contain the PIN.

The equipment for automatically inserting this data into the card is able to produce the PIN using a random number generator so that the operator does not know or see which PIN has been assigned to which card. At the same time the PIN can be printed and sealed in an envelope automatically for sending to the cardholder separately from the card. This helps to maintain security should the card fall into the wrong hands.

7 SECURITY FEATURES

ONE OF the most important features of the smart card is security. It is of primary importance in many of the applications to which the smart card can be put. For instance, when used as a medical card, the card must be able to protect sensitive data from access by unauthorised persons or, when used in financial applications, it needs to be very secure to prevent monetary fraud. Unlike passive devices, such as magnetic stripe cards, the smart card, with its on-board computing power, is able to use its 'intelligence' to counter attacks from unauthorised persons intent on fraud or on reading confidential data stored in the card. This chapter describes the security features of the smart card and how it can make a system secure.

Consider first where attacks on a system might come from. By way of example we shall use a financial application. In the example the card is to be used in a system where it acts as a secure identifying token in the electronic transfer of money from a shop's point-of-sale terminal

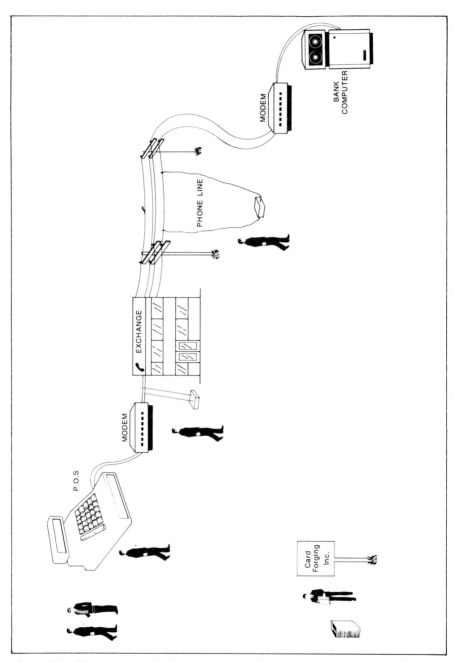

Fig. 7.1. Points at which attacks might be made on security in a financial smart card application

to a bank's computer. Attacks on the system, as shown in Fig. 7.1, can come from three principal directions:

- Forged cards could be made and used to break into the system.
- A genuine cardholder could have his card stolen and this card could be used to gain unauthorised access to the system.
- The communication lines could be tapped at various points. For example, between the point-of-sale terminal and the telephone exchange, at the telephone wires, or at the point of entry of the bank's communication lines to the computer.

Security features to prevent such attacks can be grouped under the three headings:

- Physical and manufacturing security.
- Personal identification security.
- Communications security.

Within each of these categories there are a number of routes of attack open to the fraudster and the measures to counteract these are described in the following sections. The whole area of security is very complex and the aim of this chapter is only to present in a simple and non-technical manner the measures that the smart card offers to prevent fraud. For a more detailed explanation the reader is referred to the many books that have been written on the subject of computer security.

PHYSICAL AND MANUFACTURING SECURITY

Smart cards are very difficult to reproduce without the right facilities and expertise. Manufacture of the chips requires very complex and expensive equipment – not the type of equipment that could easily be obtained by a 'small-time' criminal and set up in a back room for the manufacture of fake cards. Even if stolen chips are used, their bonding to the substrates and their encapsulation into the card both require specialised equipment. Custom chips for smart cards are not publicly available and would not be easy to obtain. Also, any attempt to decipher the contents of a chip from an existing card would, at least, need access to an electron microscope.

In addition, the expertise required to produce the cards is by no means trivial. It has taken highly qualified technical experts a number of years to develop and perfect the manufacturing processes and it would require technically knowledgeable and very competent fraudsters to have any chance of producing the fake cards.

Another approach that could be taken by the fraudster would be to learn the secrets of the card by probing its memory, then substituting the card with a device that could masquerade as the card. This, however, is extremely difficult. The first obstacle to this form of attack is presented by the packaging. Unlike many standard electronic products where the outer casing can be detached and the electronics inside probed, contactless smart cards, for instance, are entirely encapsulated, preventing any access to the electronics. Any attempt to get through this packaging can, in itself, cause damage to the chips, making it pointless to proceed.

The most secure smart cards have both the memory and the microprocessor on the same chip. Where they are separate devices it could be possible to X-ray the card and ascertain the positions of the communication lines between the two. By careful probing through the outer layers of the card it could be possible to read out the information flowing between the microprocessor and memory. However, it is virtually impossible to extract this information from smart cards that have the microprocessor and memory combined on the same chip.

Another form of attack could be to use a scanning electron microscope to read the contents of memory. However, according to experts at the UK's National Physical Laboratory, the beam from the electron microscope has the effect of erasing the contents of EEPROM memory. So cards incorporating this type of memory are additionally secure.

Having come to the conclusion that it is extremely difficult to manufacture fraudulent cards the fraudster may then turn his attention to stealing cards from a legitimate manufacturer. Producing cards is, today, very much like printing money. It is carried out in a secure environment with closed circuit television cameras continually surveying the scene, alarms and highly secure storage areas, surrounded by wall and floors of very thick concrete. In addition, a secure audit trail is usually in place so that all material, chips and so on, that enter the manufacturing plant can be accounted for at any stage. This includes all scrap and failed parts.

Yet another approach the fraudster might make would be to steal cards after they have left the manufacturing plant and before they are issued. With the correct equipment it could, conceiveably be possible to reprogram a card which held its program in EEPROM and personalise it with fraudulent data. However, most cards hold their operating system in ROM and the application program can also be held there if a high level of security is required. ROM is irrevocably fixed at the chip manufacturing stage and cannot be altered thereafter even by the manufacturer.

Personalising a stolen card cannot be achieved without the correct personalising key – a sequence of characters that must be entered. If an incorrect key is entered the card will not talk at all or, if it does, any transmitted data will be unintelligible to anybody not possessing the key. The key and the cards follow separate paths to the issuer so that, even if the cards are stolen, they cannot be issued unless the key has also been obtained.

Issuers also impose the discipline that no one person is able to carry out the complete personalising process. This helps to safeguard against fraud by potentially dishonest banking employees.

PERSONAL IDENTIFICATION SECURITY

The second category of security concerns the linking of the card to its rightful owner. In the hypothetical system, outlined at the beginning of this chapter, there was a security threat from someone stealing a card from the owner and presenting it at the system for personal gain. Currently, for magnetic stripe cards, the most commonly used method of identifying the owner of a card is the PIN. The card is entered into the system, the identity number stored on the card is read by the system and the PIN is generated from it by an algorithm. This is compared with the PIN typed in on a keypad by the person who presented the card. If the two agree then it is assumed that the person presenting the card is the genuine owner of the card. Alternatively, the PIN may be stored in the host computer instead of having an algorithmic link with the identity number.

Where PINs are used, the smart card offers four distinct advantages over magnetic stripe cards:

- As it has computing power the smart card can carry out the PIN comparison itself and does not have to reveal its identity number to the system, thus avoiding a security weakness of the conventional system.
- The PIN that is keyed in can be encrypted and, because the smart card has intelligence, can be decrypted by the card. So, if somebody succeeds in tapping the line, the PIN cannot be read.
- The card can recognise whether a number of attempts are being

made to enter different numbers until the correct PIN is found. After a set number of attempts – three for instance – it can invalidate itself so that it cannot be used again until it is reinitialised by the card issuer. On-line magnetic stripe card systems can equally offer this feature but the number of failed attempts is stored on the system computer rather than the card. This is not a problem except where some of the card entry points are connected to a different master computer. It would then be possible to move from card entry point to card entry point, keying in numbers until the PIN was found. The smart card, on the other hand, can readily store the number of entry attempts in its own memory and, thereby, recognise that, say three, attempts have been made, even if the card is presented at different entry points.

● With a smart card the owner is able to change the issued PIN, any mumber of times, to a different one which may also be more easily remembered. The card could even be programmed to protect the user against himself by refusing to accept a PIN which is too obvious, such as 1234. With magnetic stripe cards the banking system allows only one change of PIN.

Identification, through the use of a PIN or password, can only prove that someone knows the key to the system. It does not prove that the person using the card is the authorised cardholder. So, in our example, somebody who has difficulty remembering the PIN, and has written it on the card, provides all that is necessary for the card thief to gain access to the system. To link the person positively to the card requires some additional or alternative method of personal identification.

The memory capacity of the smart card makes the use of alternatives possible. These alternatives are known as *biometrics* which involve the measurement of a unique personal characteristic of the cardholder, followed by digitisation of the measured characteristic and the recording of it in the card. Some of the characteristics being considered for this purpose are dynamic signature verification, fingerprint, voice patterns, hand geometry and retinal eye patterns (see Fig. 7.2).

The performance of biometric methods of identification is not easy to measure as the need to accept genuine subjects has to be balanced against the need to reject impostors. When a genuine subject is rejected it is referred to as a type I or false reject rate (FRR) system error, and is caused by a system which has been made too secure. A type II or false accept rate (FAR) system error occurs when an impostor is accepted, and is the result of a system which is not secure enough. The sensitivity of the system which matches the subject's registered profile to the presented subject can be adjusted to strike a balance between the two. For example, if the card is presented to support a £1,000 cheque the FRR would be set high, whereas a £1 cheque would set the FAR high.

Dynamic signature verification

Visual signature checking is the usual way in which a shopkeeper will verify the holder of a magnetic stripe card, but this method is notoriously unreliable. Very often the signature is not checked at all and, even if it is, the inspection is usually only cursory. Automatic signature verification by machine, on the other hand, is thorough, consistent, does not tire and cannot be bribed.

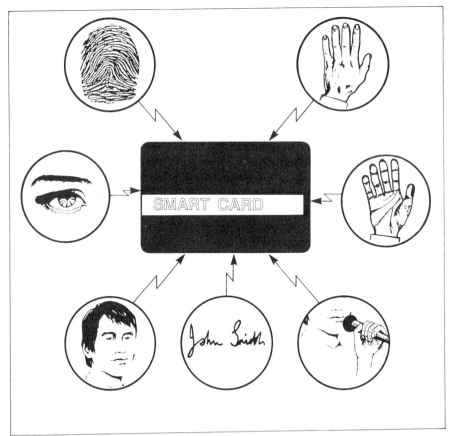

Fig. 7.2 Biometric methods for unique identificaton of the cardholder

There are two ways of checking whether a signature is genuine: dynamic, which traces the way in which the signature is written; and static, which compares the way the signature looks after it is written. Analysis of the dynamics of writing offers important and useful distinctive features for the recognition process. It is much more difficult to copy the way a signature is written than it is to copy a signature for static checking.

Systems have been developed by, among others, the National Physical Laboratory (NPL) in the UK, the Stanford Research Institute (SRI) and IBM. Each of the systems uses a different approach to the collection of dynamic signature information. The NPL system uses a digitiser, based on pressure membranes, to sample the position of the pen. The SRI system uses a ballpoint pen containing strain-gauge instruments to measure drag forces in the X and Y directions (i.e. in the plane of the writing surface) and pressure on the surface in the Z direction. SRI also developed a system based on a platen which collected the same data. The IBM system uses a pen containing accelerometers to collect data.

Another system, known as Sign/On, developed by Signify and shown in Fig. 7.3 uses a different method of data collection. It employs an electromagnetic digitiser and a wired pen with an energised coil coupled to secondary coils in the XY plane underneath the writing surface. The interaction between the pen and the writing surface means that the position of the pen can be recorded, even when it is lifted during signature writing. There is, however, a potential problem of damage through dropping or vandalism in systems which use special pens and the digitisers with pressure sensitive membranes tend to wear out.

As with all biometric identification methods, errors can be made which cause genuine subjects to be rejected and allow imposters access (see Fig. 7.2). With some signature systems the type I error rate can be as low as 1.5% and the type II error rate around 5%, although less than 1% has been claimed. Individuals with inconsistent signature patterns need not necessarily be rejected by the system as they can be asked to sign several times. An inconsistent signature can then become part of their identification.

Signature verification requires, typically, 40-200 bytes of memory.

Fingerprint verification

Everyone is familiar with the use of fingerprint identification in criminal investigations. The major features of arch, loop and whorl are clearly visible to the naked eye but it is the lesser features, known as

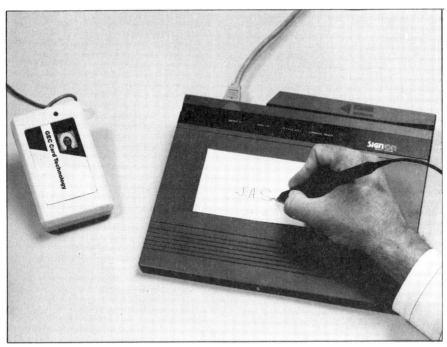

Fig. 7.3 The 'Sign/On' dynamic signature tablet can operate with the GEC contactless smart card. (Photograph courtesy of Alan Leibert Associates)

'minutiae', ridge ends and ridge bifurcations for instance, that are used for criminal identification by the police. The location and orientation of these small features are used by both manual and machine methods of verification. There are, typically, between 50 and 200 minutiae per finger and 20 are sufficient for positive identification.

Manual methods of identification include dusting areas with powder to develop prints, and taking fingerprints from suspects using an ink pad. Machine identification is usually carried out by placing the finger on a reading area where a technique, such as total internal reflection with a glass plate, is used to create an image of the print. The image is then scanned to determine the location and orientation of the minutiae. Variations in the exact positioning of the finger on the plate may make it necessary for the computer to be able to rotate the image until a best match is made.

In tests it was found that it was more difficult to identify prints in cold weather but easier with dirty, particularly greasy, fingers. There was a higher error rate for women than for men, and manual workers and people with DIY hobbies were difficult to identify. However, one system, developed in the USA by Fingermatrix and shown in Fig. 7.4 takes account of damaged fingerprints and is able to 'heal' the image so that it can still be compared with the reference image. The manufacturer claims that the type I error rate for this system is no greater than 0.1% and the type II error rate is no greater than 0.0001%.

Fingerprint identification is said to be unpopular with the public because of its association with criminal investigation. It requires, typically, between 300 and 1,000-plus bytes of memory to record a fingerprint.

One organisation, the Bank of America Card Centre in California, is already making use of a fingerprint verification unit in conjunction with a smart card. The company's employees have smart cards with three levels of security – card authentication in a reader, PIN verification and fingerprint verification. Depending upon the areas where access is being sought, the appropriate security verification is required. To allow access to the computer rooms and other sensitive areas the highest level of secure access is required. The cardholder's fingerprint is compared with a digitised print stored in the card. If the two match access is granted.

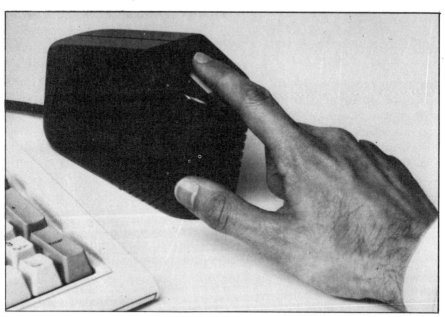

Fig. 7.4 Fingermatrix fingerprint identification system electronically scans fingerprint ridges. (Photograph courtesy of Fingermatrix)

Voice recognition

For a computer to be able to recognise a voice it has to be programmed to compare measured features of the voice with a recorded original. Typically, when first introduced to the system, a subject is asked to speak certain words and phrases into a microphone. The voice pattern is then analysed to extract the necessary information required for identification. When the subject next wishes to gain access to the system, he or she is prompted to speak selected words or phrases. The selection by the system of words or phrases to be spoken makes it more difficult for an intruder to gain access using a recording of an authorised user's voice.

Research has found that particular speaker training techniques can reduce the number of errors in voice recognition systems but factors outside the speaker's control, such as throat infections or emotional stress, can affect the voice to the extent that he or she will be rejected. Voice recognition systems tend to have a high type I error rate of up to 3% and a type II error rate of below 1% but these can be adjusted, depending on the degree of security required. Voice patterns typically use between 100 and 200 bytes of memory.

Hand geometry

Research has shown that individual hands have unique features such as finger lengths, skin web opacity and radius of curvature of fingertips. Systems have been produced which measure hand geometries by scanning with photo-electric devices. The hand is positioned on a faceplate and a capacitive switch senses the presence of the hand and initiates scanning. The measurements are then compared with previously stored data. It has been claimed that type I and II error rate is of 0.1% possible using this method.

According to a report by the National Physical Laboratory, identification using hand geometry can be of high cost and low accuracy but requires only a small amount of memory – less than 20 bytes for some systems.

Retinal pattern verification

The pattern of the blood vessels on the retina of the human eye is a unique physical characteristic. The EyeDentify Corporation of Portland, USA, has developed a device for scanning the retina and verifying identity, see Fig. 7.5. When introduced to the system, the subject's retina is scanned using a low intensity infra-red beam. The

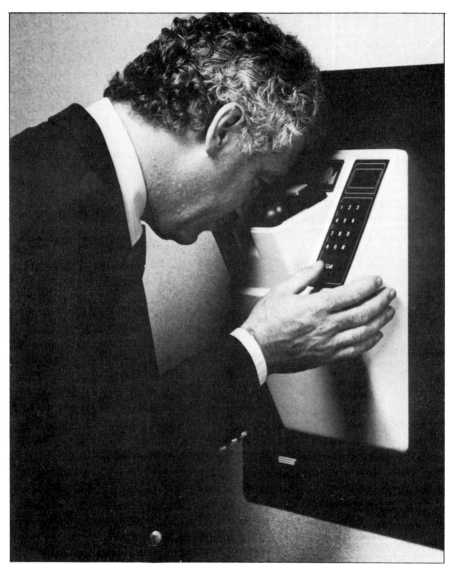

Fig. 7.5 EyeDentify retinal pattern verification system. (Photograph courtesy of EyeDentify Inc.)

scan centres on the fovea where vision is sharpest. The user is asked to focus on a daisy-like object until it changes from red to green, when the focus is correct. By taking 320 readings of light and shade the system locates the nodes and branches of the blood vessel pattern and, using their location in the annular area, forms a profile of the subject for comparison on other occasions.

This method is both fast and accurate with a very low type I error rate and a negligible type II error rate. It requires only 30-40 bytes of memory. The method may, however, meet with resistance from users.

For a comparison of the principal biometric techniques which have just been described, see Fig. 7.6.

	Typical memory requirements	Typical false acceptance
Signature	40–200 bytes	1 in hundreds
Fingerprint	300–1000+ bytes	1 in million
Voice	100–200 bytes	1 in thousands
Hand geometry	10–200 bytes	1 in thousand
Eye retinal	30–40 bytes	1 in billions

Fig. 7.6 Comparison of principal biometric identification methods

Vein pattern recognition

This method, like retinal pattern verification, uses the unique vein structure of the human body to identify individuals. In this case, it is the veins in the hand or wrist that are used. The 'veincheck' system, being developed in the UK, uses a simple infra-red scanning and encoding technique to locate the number, position and size of subcutaneous blood vessels.

Visual recognition

It is possible to digitise a picture of a person and store it in a smart card's memory. However, it does require more memory than most other biometric techniques. The picture, usually obtained by a scanning video camera, is digitised and then compressed to enable it to be stored in the smart card.

COMMUNICATIONS SECURITY

The third category of security features offered by the smart card relates to communications. To be of any use, all cards, unless they are only used for visual identification purposes, have to communicate with another device. Communications may be through a read/write unit connected to a point-of-sale terminal and telephone lines to a computer, as in our example of Fig. 7.1, or may just be with a simple read/write unit incorporating a display and keyboard. Whatever the device with which the card has to communicate, the security of messages and data being transferred is usually of prime importance. The smart card, with its processing ability, provides, for the first time in card systems, a means for end to end security.

There are four basic requirements that must be attained when messages are transmitted between a smart card and another device, if security is to be assured. They are:

- Integrity.
- Validity.
- Authenticity.
- Privacy.

By *integrity* we mean that the card and system must be able to detect whether the message that has been sent between the two has been altered deliberately or accidentally. *Validity* refers to unauthorised recordings of genuine messages that are played back at a later date for gain by the fraudster. *Authenticity* refers to the ability of the card and system to determine that messages are being received from a genuine sender and sent to a genuine receiver. *Privacy* refers to the ability to prevent unauthorised persons from reading the messages that are being transmitted.

To understand more fully what is meant by integrity, authenticity, validity and privacy, it helps to draw an analogy with the sending and receiving of a letter through the post. The integrity of the letter can be ascertained by the receiver by visual inspection – to see if modifications have been made to the letter. The addition of redundancy also helps to ensure integrity. A letter referring to a sum of money may have both numerals and a value in written English – £500 (five hundred pounds only). This ensures, for example, that if one of the zeros is not typed (making the £500 into £50) it will be detected by the recipient of the letter when that person reads the words which follow the typed numbers.

Writing the date on the letter ensures its validity. For instance, three relatives may have letters from a deceased person stating how his estate should be divided upon his death. Each relative may claim that the letter which benefits him most is the letter which the deceased intended as the statement of how his possessions should be divided. It is, in fact, the letter with the most current date which defines which letter is valid. In the same way, the date franking of the envelope in which the letter is sent also helps to determine its validity.

Authenticity of a letter is usually ensured by the handwritten signature at the bottom of the letter which can be visually recognised by the receiver. Official letter headings also help to ensure authenticity.

Privacy is obtained by inserting the letter in an envelope and sealing it. The receiver, upon inspection of the envelope, can usually see if it has been illicitly opened. Centuries ago, privacy of written documents was assured using a seal of molten wax with the imprint of an official stamp. The breaking of the seal, by someone intent on reading the message, could be detected by the person for whom the message was intended.

How, then, can the equivalence of these security features in a letter be transposed into security features for communications between a smart card and another device?

Integrity

A traditional technique for ensuring integrity of data is the checksum. A checksum is a method by which the individual bits that make up a message are summed. This summation is appended to the message to be transmitted. The receiver of the message can carry out the same summation of bits in the received message and check them against the transmitted checksum. If the two correspond then the message has not been altered, accidentally or otherwise, in transmission. There are weaknesses in the traditional checksum but a more secure use of it is discussed later.

Validity

If a genuine message that, for example, credits a person's bank account with £50 can be recorded by a fraudster it could, potentially, be continually replayed, each time adding £50 to that person's bank account. Validity can be provided in various ways but all ensure that, in some way, each message that is sent is unique. Any subsequent identical message, for example a recorded message, can then be assumed to be fraudulent. The uniqueness can be obtained by adding the date and time when it is sent, by adding a number which increments with each message that is sent or by generating a random number each time a message is to be sent and appending it to that message. Clearly, when the unique numbers are sent as part of a message they must be transmitted in a form that cannot be recognised or altered by the fraudster.

Authenticity

To ensure that the card and receiving device are communicating with each other, rather than with a fraudulent device inserted in the communication path, it is possible to use a combination of the checksum and the attachment of a random number to the message. The checksum, in this case, is produced in a much more complex way because of the ease with which the previous method allowed the fraudster to generate a valid checksum. It is a one-way operation, being impossible to work backwards from the result. This more secure method involves use of an algorithm, known as the *authenticator*, and a secret key. These are held only by the genuine receiver and sender of messages. Without knowledge of the authenticator algorithm or the secret key, the checksum cannot be generated or verified. The method is such that any alteration of a bit of data affects the checksum in an unpredictable manner.

To ensure message authenticity, both the smart card and the receiving device have, embedded in them, an identical authentication algorithm and secret keys. The card first generates a random number, R_1, and sends it to the receiving device (see Fig. 7.7 (a)). Both the receiver and the smart card process the random number with the authentication algorithm and secret key. The receiving device then sends the result, $A (K, R_1)$, back to the smart card which compares it with the result it has generated. If the two match then the smart card knows that the receiving device is authentic. However, at this stage the receiving device does not yet know whether the card is authentic. It determines this by generating its own random number R_2 which it transmits to the smart card at the same time as it sends the result of the previously processed random number back to the card (see Fig. 7.7 (b) (b)). Both card and receiving device then process this new random number and the card sends the result, $A(K, R_2)$, back to the receiving device, (see Fig. 7.7 (c)). If this matches the result obtained by the receiving device then it deems the card authentic.

Messages containing the data to be transmitted are only sent after this initial procedure of three transmissions has taken place. As far as the fraudster is concerned he sees only random and pseudo-random numbers passing along the lines. With a random number of sufficient

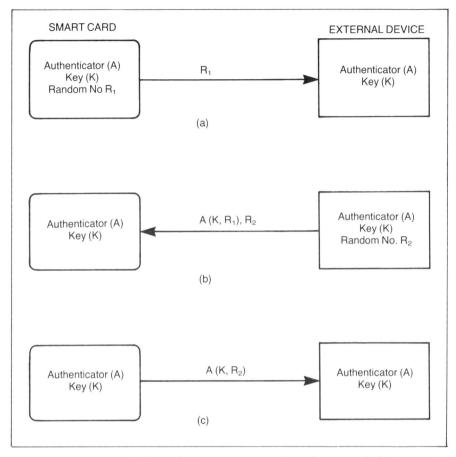

Fig. 7.7 The principle by which a smart card and external device each detemine the authenticity of the other

length the chances of guessing the right number is remote. After this initial sequence, messages can be securely sent, each one with a random number to ensure its uniqueness and an authentication code forming the special checksum. In this way message integrity, validity and authenticity are achieved.

Privacy

Privacy is ensured using encryption, also known as encipherment or scrambling of data. Encryption is defined as a method whereby the data to be transmitted is made unintelligible, using a set of rules, is transmitted in the unintelligible form and is reconstituted into readable form, by the receiver, using a related set of rules.

Encryption, by substitution of one set of characters for another using a table of substitutions and the moving of characters around within a message, goes back a number of years. Originally it was carried out manually and, later, with the help of computers. During the Second World War computers were first used to help with the breaking of encryption codes. It was also during the war that Shannon established the mathematical foundations of information theory and applied it to encryption. He concluded that a good encryption algorithm should contain both substitutions and transpositions of text and required a long key.

During the 1960s IBM, which had an increasing need for security features in its products, initiated research into encryption. One such method, based on Shannon's work, was adopted in the early 1970s by the National Bureau of Standards, part of the US Department of Commerce. Encryption systems until that time had, generally, been for military or diplomatic use and were kept secret. However, the National Bureau of Standards published the method that they had adopted for use outside these circles and it became known as the Data Encryption Standard (DES). It consists of a published algorithm, which defines the procedure for encrypting, and keys, which provide the uniqueness for the encryption. The keys are 56 bits long and data is encrypted in blocks of 64 bits.

Publication of an encryption algorithm may seem to be a contradiction in terms. However, the security of the system relies on the fact that the only way of cracking it is by comparing an unencoded message (referred to as plain text) with an encoded message (cypher text), and by trying all possible keys. Using 56 bits for the key, means that the number of different keys possible is just short of one hundred thousand million million. Even if it took only one millionth of a second for a computer to test for each of the keys it would still take the computer 2,000 years to test for all of the keys. By using 1,000,000 computers, carrying out tests in parallel, the time to test for all keys could be reduced to 10 hours, but the cost of the million computers, the room they would take up and the chances of all of them running for 10 hours without error makes it impractical to crack DES encryption messages.

Combining authentication and encryption

A method for combining the authentication method, described previously with DES encryption to produce secure communications between the card and receiving device is illustrated in Fig. 7.8. The message to be sent is first encrypted using the DES algorithm and secret key. As DES encryption is not particularly fast in a smart card, any part of the message which is not confidential may be left unencrypted. A header is then constructed. This comprises a random number generated by the card, the card's identity so that the receiver knows which card has sent the information, the receiver's identity to confirm that it is the receiver for whom the message is intended and the last random number generated by a receiver (not necessarily the same one). After construction the header is appended to the message and the two are processed with the authentication algorithm and its secret key to form an authentication code. The header, message and authentication code can then be transmitted securely to the receiving device. At the receiver the authenticator is stripped off and checked. Then the header is stripped off and checked before the message is accepted.

Problems with DES encryption

One of the problems with DES encryption is that it relies on the use of the same key for encryption as for decryption. In a system where there are a number of different users, each pairing requires a unique key which must be kept secret. It is advisable to change these keys frequently and the process of generating, issuing and protection of the keys is known as key management. Key management is by no means a small task if there are a number of communicating pairs distributed over a wide geographic area.

Problems can also arise with the use of DES if one of the participants of a pair is intent on fraud. For instance, company A may be required to transmit a sum of £1,000 owed to company B. However, company A is going through a period of financial difficulty so transmits only £100, encrypted using the DES algorithm and key. However, having the algorithm and key, company A is able to generate a message, which is not transmitted but is stored in its computer, which states that £1,000 was transmitted. Company B is naturally unhappy with receiving £900 less than was due so, having checked that its transmitting and receiving equipment is functioning correctly, telephones company A demanding the missing money. Company A claims, however, that £1,000 was sent, that the evidence is stored in its computer and that there is also nothing wrong with its transmitting and receiving equipment. It then counter-claims that company B has changed the amount to £100 and, by using the same algorithm and key, has produced a new valid message for use as evidence. If this case

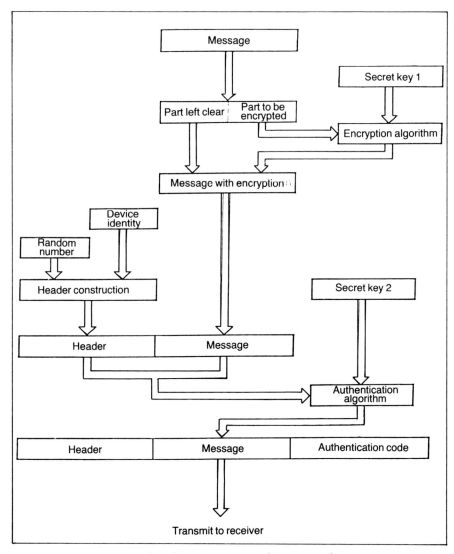

Fig. 7.8 Encryption and authentication combine to make a message secure

went to a law court, there would be no way in which anything could be proved, as both parties would have valid messages as evidence. This situation is made possible because both parties have the same algorithm and key.

The principal problems with DES are, therefore, connected with key management, the need to keep the encryption key secret and the problems that arise in cases of dispute.

RSA public key encryption

DES is known as a symmetrical cypher – that is, the encryption key and decryption key are the same. However, there are systems using what is known as *public key encryption* where the encryption and decryption keys are different and which require only one of the keys to be kept secret. The other key can be made public. Such a method was postulated in 1976 by Whitfield Diffie and Martin Hellman. One year later, the RSA public key encryption scheme was invented by Rivest, Shamir and Adleman, working at the Massachusetts Institute of Technology, USA. (The name RSA is, in fact, formed from the first letter of each of the inventors' names).

The security of RSA is based on the difficulty of factorising the product of two very large prime numbers. There is a relationship between the secret and public keys which can be exploited by the communicating devices in the system but which does not allow the secret key to be inferred from the public key.

Consider how the RSA technique can be applied to ensure secrecy of communications between a smart card, A, and another device, B. The procedure for secure communications using RSA can be simplified into two stages:

- *Stage 1.* A uses its secret key S_A to encrypt; B decrypts the message using A's public key P_A that is, $A (S_A) \rightarrow B (P_A)$. There are two important points to be noted: only A could have sent the message because it is the only unit with the secret key; and all devices with A's public key can receive the message. In other words, using the letter analogy, only one person can generate the signed letter (secret key) but a number of people can check the received letter against a reference signature (public key).
- *Stage 2.* A uses B's public key, P_B, to encrypt the message; B decrypts the message using its secret key S_B; that is, $A (P_B) \rightarrow B (S_B)$. The points that stand out here are: any device could have transmitted the message; and only B could have decrypted the message because it alone has the secret key.

Stage 1, therefore, defines the single unit that could have sent the message while Stage 2 defines the one unit that can receive the message. By combining stage 1 and stage 2 we get: $A (S_A, P_B) \rightarrow B (S_B, P_A)$. In other words, A first uses its secret key to encrypt the message, and then encrypts the result using B's public key before transmitting the message. To decrypt the message B first uses its secret key to decrypt the received message and then applies A's public key to fully decrypt the message.

The result obtained from this technique is a precise definition of the unique sender (an electronic signature) and the ability to send the message to a defined unit only while making widely known the public key. In this way it is possible to resolve the dispute described earlier between company A and company B where each is accusing the other of fraud. At the same time the problem of key management – the distribution of keys – is also overcome as public keys for each company can be published in a directory and widely distributed without compromising security.

RSA, as we have seen, offers several advantages over DES. However, the amount of computation required to execute RSA makes it impractical for today's smart cards. The microprocessors currently employed in smart cards would require several minutes to encrypt a 512-bit block of data. Devices such as the NPL token described in Chapter 5, which incorporate special chips, are able to use RSA and it may be only a matter of time before smart cards have the memory capacity and speed necessary to execute RSA.

This leads to another public key encryption method, known as the Fiat Shamir technique, which was devised by Fiat and Shamir (Shamir is the S of the RSA collaboration) at the Weismann Institute of Science in Israel, and which was first published in May 1986. It is based on a technique known as zero knowledge proof. The advantages of this method over RSA are that it is much faster to execute and it does not require as much program memory. It is a relatively new method which may well become prominent in smart card applications.

8

FINANCIAL
APPLICATIONS

THE WORLD of finance – banking, insurance, wholesale and retail
business and so on – is one of the major application areas for smart
cards and many areas of finance will be revolutionised by the
introduction of smart cards in the future. Several different types of
financial applications are described in this chapter and many of these
can be combined on one card. There are already a number of terminals
for financial transactions which accept smart cards, and one is
illustrated in Fig. 8.1.

SOME PRINCIPAL USES

DEBIT AND CREDIT CARDS

The security features of the smart card, which were reviewed in
Chapter 7, make it ideal for use as a credit or debit card because of the

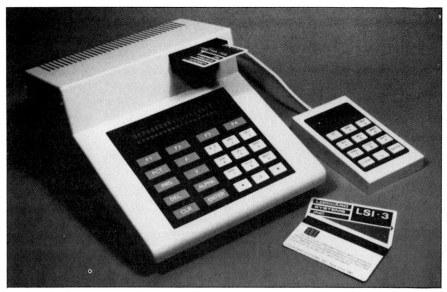

Fig. 8.1. A smart card point-of-sale terminal. (Photograph courtesy of Logicard Systems Inc.)

protection it gives against fraud. It is estimated that fraud and bad debt losses on conventional credit cards will be around $2,000m per annum by 1990 for one major card issuer alone. Fraud losses, such as use of stolen cards or altering and cloning cards, will amount to $200m, the remaining $1,800m being bad debt losses.

Dealing with bad debt losses has more to do with the policies of the issuing banks than with card technology. However, the smart card can assist in reducing bad debt losses. If the card has a built in credit limit determined by the issuer, the cardholder will be unable to exceed the limit and run up large bills which he is later unable to pay. The credit limit could be changed at a bank when the bill is paid.

When used in a financial application, the card can hold in its memory such things as:

- Cardholder's identification.
- Card issuer identification.
- Cardholder's PIN.
- Account balance.
- Transaction limit.
- Log of transactions.

ELECTRONIC CHEQUE

The smart card can be used during EFTPOS transactions – Electronic Fund Transfer at the Point-of-Sale. At a retailer's check-out the card is placed on or in the reader, where it automatically goes through authentication sequences. To authorise payment, the customer types in the PIN which the card then matches with the one held in its memory. If the number corresponds, the card will authorise the terminal to transfer funds from the cardholder's bank account to the retailer's bank account (see Fig. 8.2(a)). This can be done instantaneously, or at a pre-set time, or the transaction can be stored in the point-of-sale terminal until the terminal is interrogated by the bank's computer. A record of the transaction will be stored in the card at the same time.

The card cannot give the cardholder information about the balance in his bank account, because of other transactions such as direct debits, but it will allow transactions up to a certain limit set by the bank, perhaps on a monthly basis. This use of the smart card will bring about a significant decrease in the number of cheques and vouchers handled by financial institutions and should, therefore, reduce the costs of paper processing. On-line communications costs will also be reduced as the card's built-in authorisation means that referral to the bank's main computer is not required for every transaction. They can be batched up for transfer, for example, in the middle of the night. The ability of the smart card to contain a pre-set credit limit will reduce losses due to bad debt and will enable the financial institutions to issue cards to a greater number of people. This will, in turn, benefit the retailer as there will be more customers with credit.

ELECTRONIC TRAVELLERS' CHEQUES

The smart card can be used as a more secure and convenient replacement for travellers' cheques as depicted in Fig. 8.2(b). A pre-paid monetary value is stored in the card, possibly in a foreign currency. When payment is authorised, by the cardholder's PIN, the purchase value is deducted from the card. Reconciliation of the travellers' cheques held in the terminal will be carried out at a later date.

ELECTRONIC CASH (ELECTRONIC PURSE)

Funds can be loaded into a card for use as cash. This electronic cash

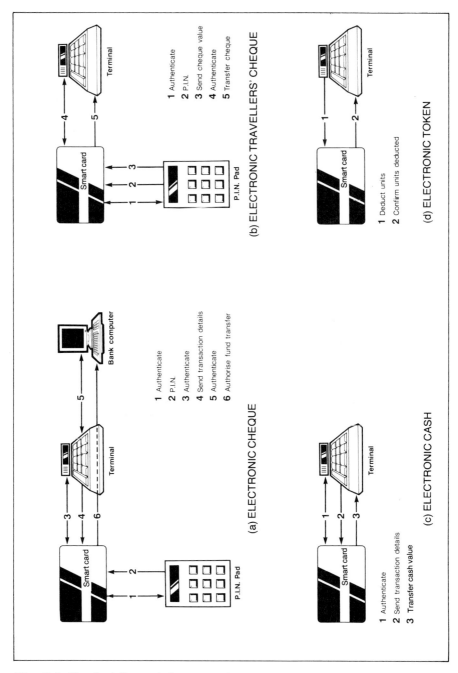

Fig. 8.2. Typical financial transactions using a smart card

can then be used for small purchases without necessarily requiring the authorisation of a PIN, (see Fig. 8.2(c)). When the card is credited with the cash the cardholder's account is debited in the normal way, except that the amount debited is then held by the bank until reclaimed by a retailer. When the card is used to purchase goods or services the value of the transaction is deducted from the card and held securely at the retailer's terminal. The retailer then presents this information to the bank so that his account can be credited. In the intervening time the bank can invest the money.

Electronic cash transactions do not usually require the use of a PIN. This speeds up the transaction but means that electronic cash is as vulnerable to theft as conventional cash. The amounts involved, however, are usually only small. Widespread adoption of electronic cash will reduce the costs to banks and retailers of handling large quantities of cash.

ELECTRONIC TOKEN

The smart card has considerable potential as an electronic token, possibly in association with other uses. The principle here is that a pre-paid area is set aside to store electronic units of time or electronic tickets, etc., for a specific service or item, (see Fig. 8.2(d)). Magnetic stripe cards are currently being used extensively with public tele-phones, parking meters and vending machines for this type of application. At present these are discarded when empty. However, a smart card can be used to combine several token areas and each of these could be recharged, depending on the type of memory in the card. This allows the cost to be distributed over a number of services and over a much longer issue life.

For example, the card could be used to pay for gas and electricity as a replacement for coin meters. Consumers could pay for units at a vending machine at the gas or electricity company shop, which would credit their cards. The cards would then be used to operate the meters. The advantages of this system would be that collections would no longer have to be made and there would be no incentive for people to rob meters or collectors. There would also be benefits for the consumer as units could be bought and stored in the card in advance, in a similar way to buying telephone stamps, for instance. The card could, conceivably, be identified with one particular meter so that it would not operate another. It is possible that the card could also monitor patterns of use and give back information on peak consumption times so that the consumer could make savings.

The first steps towards using smart cards as electronic tokens, are already being taken, as shown in Fig. 8.3, and it will not be long before they operate as multiple token cards.

CORPORATE CASH MANAGEMENT SERVICES

Banks are now beginning to provide corporate cash management services to companies and major clients. In this area smart cards can act as secure keys allowing major account holders access to the bank's mainframe computers to view their accounts and transfer money automatically between accounts.

Fig. 8.3. A vending machine operated by smart cards. (Photograph courtesy of Mitsubishi)

SHARE DEALING

The inherent security of the smart card makes it useful in a wider field of financial applications. Trading of stocks and shares, for instance, can be controlled by using the card to limit access to trading terminals and to log bargains made. Data could later be transferred from the card to a stock exchange settlement computer.

ALLOWANCES AND PENSIONS

The smart card is ideal as a medium for the payment of family allowances, social security allowances (welfare) and pensions. It could be used in these applications to alleviate much of the paper processing required at the moment.

SOME INTERNATIONAL EXAMPLES

In FRANCE trials have been run using smart card payment systems. Between January 1983 and June 1984 a test of smart cards was run, simultaneously, in the towns of Blois, Caen and Lyons. Different cards were used in each town – Honeywell Bull cards in Blois, Philips cards in Caen and Flonic Schlumberger cards in Lyons. The banks participating in the trial had enquiry terminals where cardholders could check their accounts and read their transaction records for the current month or for the card's entire history.

There were 463 points-of-sale equipped to read the smart cards. When a purchase was made, the retailer inserted the card into the terminal, entered the amount and depressed the 'Telebank' key. The customer then keyed in the PIN and collected a receipt. Data was then passed from the point-of-sale terminal to a data collection machine. The smart card system was generally favoured by retailers although there was some dispute over fees levied by the banks for use of the system.

In July 1984, the national organisation Groupement Carte Bancaire, reached a decision to expand and develop the use of smart cards and to unify the two existing rival groups, Carte Bleue and Carte Verte, to form 'Carte Bancaire'. The reasons for the decision to continue were that:

● Smart card technology had been proved successful and had the potential to prevent fraud

- There could be a smooth change-over from existing magnetic stripe cards as smart cards could work with existing readers.
- Communications between the card and the reader could be encrypted to increase security.

The banks have since announced that by 1990 payment by smart card will be general all over France. The first areas to be covered by this generalisation are Rennes, Marseille, Lyon and Paris. Bull CP8 is supplying 12 million cards and Philips is supplying 4 million.

A trial was run in Bormio, ITALY, in January and February 1985 and ran for 45 days, the duration of the World Downhill Ski Championships which were held in Bormio that year. The trial was promoted by a local bank with 30 branches, Credito Valtellinese, and Enidata, a software house. The smart card used was called 'Tellcard' and could be used in 31 shops in Bormio including sports shops, grocers, clothing shops and restaurants, among others. The card was issued to 4,500 people. Interestingly, 44% of the transactions were for food although only 23% of shops participating were food outlets.

In the UNITED STATES, Mastercard have been involved in trials of smart cards. The objective of one of the trials in Florida was to test smart cards in automated self-service supermarket check-outs.

In NEW ZEALAND a smart card, launched by Asset Card Ltd, gave the cardholder access to a Mastercard credit card, an Asset working account, which operated in the same way as an interest-bearing cheque account, and a Post Bank account nominated by the cardholder, which allowed direct debit for EFTPOS purchases. Consumers paid $7.50 per month for the use of the card, and this included subscription for Mastercard. The card could be used at L. D. Nathan stores – Woolworth, Big City Stores, Electric City and James Smith.

Citibank, in the UNITED KINGDOM, issued smart cards to clients wishing to transfer large funds of more than $100,000 from one country to another. The effect of this is similar to travellers' cheques as it allows cardholders to draw money in local currency in Citibank branches abroad.

In a rather similar type of application a LUXEMBOURG bank, Credit Europeen, is to replace 40,000 magnetic stripe cards with smart cards. The cards in question are based on the European Currency Unit (ECU) and are issued in association with Visa International. The bank will initially only issue its smart card in Luxembourg and France, but the bank hopes to be able to extend use of the card to cover all the European Community eventually.

In the NETHERLANDS, a smart card test commenced in 1985, in a petrol payment application, in the North Brabant region and in the town of Tilburg. The trial was run by the commercial banks and took three years to set up. Eighty-four petrol stations run by nine oil companies were involved.

In JAPAN a vending machine operated by smart cards, has been developed jointly by Nippon Coinco Company and Kyowa Bank. The transactions are recorded on a smart card in the machine for payment into the bank at a later time.

The Royal Bank of CANADA (RBC) is using smart cards in its on-line corporate cash-management system. Readers and cards have been distributed to customers for use with IBM-compatible personal computers. The smart card holds the corporate customer's self-selected PIN and the company telephone number. Customers have a choice of either transferring their management data to the RBC system using the bank's own software known as Cashcommand, or down-loading information from the bank to be used with commercially available software such as Lotus 1-2-3. RBC has protected its software by putting some of the instructions for the program on to the smart card so that it will only run with the card in place. Smart card access has also been extended to the clients' payrolls, letters of credit and asset and debt management. The smart card system has the benefit of being highly secure as well as reducing communications and comput-ing costs to the user and the bank.

Stockbroking and stock transfer services can be accessed in SWITZERLAND by customers of Credit Suisse, using personal computers in their own offices. Security of the system is assured by a personalised smart card, which carries the customer's identity and other details, and which is inserted into a card reader attached to the personal computer. Credit Suisse charges a monthly fee of SwFr3,000 and issues the card and reader to the customer. A highly secure algorithmic identity procedure is employed for mutual verification, and the procedure is repeated at each stage in the transaction.

In JAPAN the Mitsui Bank has run a trial involving smart cards in a corporate banking system. The cards were used to identify personnel authorised to access and move funds on-line to Mitsui Bank.

Smart cards are also being introduced into home banking services. In Japan, for instance, the New Media Services (NMS) group with the Sumito Bank and 16 other organisations are working on a home banking system which uses a videotext system. A trial involving 1,000 people will cover deposit balance checking and alteration, as well as data transmission.

CASE STUDIES

THE MIDLAND BANK TRIAL AT LOUGHBOROUGH UNIVERSITY

In October 1988 the Midland Bank began an experiment in smart card technology at Loughborough University in the UK. The card is known as the MeritCard and is a contactless smart card developed by GEC Card Technology. A University was chosen for the experiment because it offers an excellent controlled environment for the distribution of cards and is, effectively, a microcosm of a typical British town – having its own bank, bars, shops and restaurants, serving about 5,000 students. It was also chosen in the belief that the security of the system would be thoroughly tested by students who might have the technical knowledge and facilities to be tempted to try to break into the system.

Students at the university are able to use the card to pay for any purchases made at the university shops, restaurants and bars, as well as to gain access to information services which would not normally be available on the campus. The system installed at the university is shown in Fig. 8.4.

Card issuing station

Anyone with a current account held at the Midland Bank's Loughborough University branch can apply for a MeritCard. When the application form is completed it is sent to the Loughborough High Street branch of the Bank where there is a card issuing station. This piece of equipment consists of a personal computer connected to two couplers (read/write units), an audit printer and a PIN mailer printer.

To issue a card, the issuing station has to be activated using a high memory capacity smart card which is placed on one of the couplers. The member of staff then enters a password to gain access to the issuing computer. The option 'new card' is then chosen from a menu and a smart card, which has not yet been personalised, is placed on the other coupler. The cardholder's details, such as name and bank account number, are entered into the computer which transmits this information through the coupler to the card for storage. The PIN is generated at the same time and is automatically printed out on a security PIN mailer. When this process is finished, the computer tells the operator that personalisation is complete. Mailers and cards are then sent to the university branch.

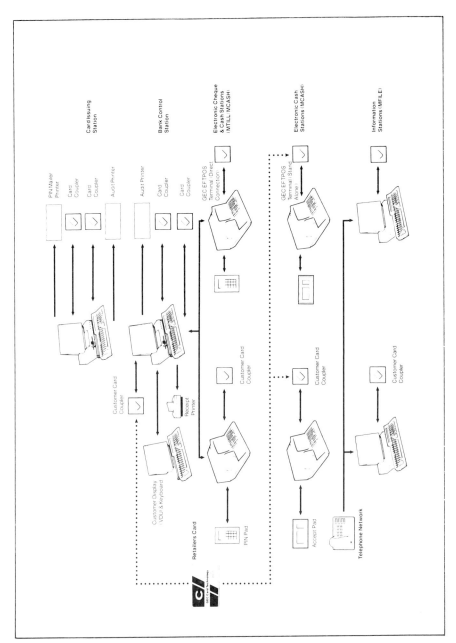

Fig. 8.4. Schematic diagram of the GEC/Midland Bank contactless smart card system tested at Loughborough University. (Diagram courtesy of GEC)

The cardholder collects the new card from the bank, and for security reasons, the PIN is posted separately to the cardholder's home address. The cardholder's first task is to go to the unmanned station in the bank (part of the control station) and change the PIN to one of his own choosing – the card will not operate until the number is changed. The cardholder can then opt to load the card with electronic cash – an electronic representation of a sum of money.

Bank control station

The main branch of the bank on campus has a bank control station which consists of a controlling computer in the bank connected to a remote screen, keyboard, receipt printer and coupler on the customer side, as in Fig. 8.4. If the station is not in use, the customer can put his card on the coupler and the screen and keyboard will become active. The customer can then choose to load electronic cash, or *MCash* as it is known, unload MCash, or change the PIN. When the customer has finished, either another customer or a bank employee can use the station.

Members of staff have to use a higher memory capacity smart card to activate the station from the bank side. They can then read details on the customer's card and print out a statement of his transactions if required. If the cardholder has had three failed attempts at the PIN, the card will have become invalid. However, staff can re-validate the card using the bank control station.

The controlling computer is also directly linked to a number of EFTPOS units. At a set time all EFTPOS units that are on-line are polled, in turn, and are asked to transfer the transactions for the day. The computer then carries out the end-of-the-day processing and produces a report of the day's work.

Very little staff training is needed to use the bank station. The system was designed to be simple to use and members of staff only need to remember the passwords. All the functions are chosen from menus displayed on the screen.

The EFTPOS units

The card is accepted at all shops, bars and restaurants on the campus which have been provided with GEC Sentinel EFTPOS units, connected to card couplers and either a PIN pad with display or an accept pad with display.

There are eight stand-alone EFTPOS units which only accept

MCash. These units also operate with a high memory capacity (retailer) smart card which is thicker than the customer's card. At the end of the day, the retailer puts this card on to the coupler and a record of the day's card transactions is transferred to it. The card is then taken to the bank, with the cash, in the normal way. At the bank, transaction records are loaded into the bank's computer from the retailer's card and the latest hot card file, containing the numbers of cards suspended or reported lost, is loaded into the retailer's smart card which is then used to transfer the information back to the retailer's EFTPOS unit.

There are four EFTPOS units located in the Students' Union building and these are hard wired directly to the bank control computer (see Fig. 8.4). The units can accept both MCash and *MTill* transactions, as described in the next section. A high memory capacity card is not required here because, at the end of the day, the card transactions are sent down the wire directly into the controlling computer in the bank. If the hot card file is changed during the day, bank staff can send the amendment immediately to each connected EFTPOS unit. The retailer, too, can contact the controlling computer at any time during the day if, for instance, he wishes to pass over his EFTPOS transactions for the day and finish trading early.

There are security features built into the cards and the EFTPOS units enabling them to verify each other's identity. When a card is placed on the coupler, the unit first checks the card's number against the hot card file. If the card is not on the file, it then sends out challenges to make sure that the EFTPOS unit is genuine. Each challenge from a card is encrypted and is different every time. If the response from the EFTPOS unit is incorrect, the card will refuse to continue. This process is repeated by the EFTPOS unit which, similarly, sends a different challenge each time to a card.

Two of the four Sentinels connected directly to the bank can also be used for boosting the MCash value of a card. If the EFTPOS unit in a shop is not busy, the cardholder can place the card on the panel. The retailer presses the MLoad button on the EFTPOS unit and the customers enters their PIN on the PIN pad and the amount of MCash required. By making it possible to load MCash in various places, queues at the bank station can be kept to a minimum.

The Meritcard

In financial transactions the MeritCard can be used in two ways: either as electronic cash, known as MCash, or as a cheque book, known as MTill.

MCash is an electronic replacement for cash. When the cardholder wishes to load the card with electronic cash, the card is placed on the panel of the appropriate terminal and the cardholder can choose to transfer up to £20 to the card from his current account. The card can be recharged as many times as required, as long as certain conditions are satisfied.

For MTill, the weekly spending limit is £100 and, as the MTill amount left decreases in relation to any MCash increase, the number of times a cardholder can recharge the card depends on how many MTill transactions have been carried out and the value of the other MCash loads in that week.

When a customer chooses to pay for goods with MCash, the operator presses the MCash payment button on the EFTPOS unit (see Fig. 8.5) and the customer liquid crystal display (LCD) screen invites the customer to place the card on the panel. After a couple of seconds, the screen will show the amount to be paid and the customer presses the accept key on the key pad. The money is then deducted from the card's balance and a record of the transaction is stored in both the card and the EFTPOS unit. For MCash transactions the cardholder's PIN is not required.

In theory, if the card is lost or stolen, MCash is no more secure than conventional cash. However, for the purposes of this experiment, the Midland Bank has added two extra features which increase the security of MCash. First, each EFTPOS unit checks the card number against the hot card list before commencing the transaction. Second, during this trial, records of all MeritCard transactions are collected by the bank, including each MCash transaction. In a nationwide application this would not be feasible as it would mean keeping too many records; each EFTPOS unit would, probably, just present the bank with the total amount of MCash collected for the day.

MTill transactions can be carried out at the four EFTPOS units with direct connections to the bank. Using MTill is the same process as writing a cheque. It will lead to a debit of the cardholder's current account and can be used for larger amounts than MCash. When the customer chooses to pay for goods with MTill, the routine is the same as for MCash except that instead of pressing the accept button, the customer has to enter his PIN. The card checks the PIN and, if it finds the PIN to be correct, the transaction is completed with records stored in the card and the EFTPOS unit.

Fig. 8.5. Paying for goods with a smart card at Loughborough University. (Photograph courtesy of GEC)

Viewdata information station

There are three viewdata information stations, known as *MFile* stations, located in the library, the students' union office and the bank. These can be used to give cardholders information about card status and to gain access to Prestel and Thomas Cook travel services.

The equipment, as shown in Fig. 8.6, consists of a Tandata PA workstation with a high resolution, compact, 12in., colour monitor and a GEC card coupler. The PA workstation has new software written for this application. It is connected to the smart card coupler, via its

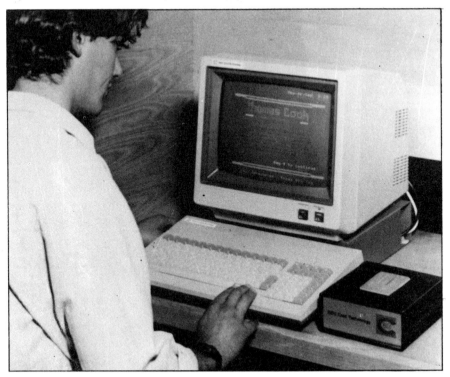

Fig. 8.6. Viewing information at a viewdata terminal which is operated by smart cards. (Photograph courtesy of GEC)

RS-232 port, and to the telephone line. The workstation uses an internal, V21/V23 multibaud rate, auto-dial modem connected to the telephone line.

The maker of the workstation, Tandata, summarise the benefits of using a smart card in a Prestel environment as follows:

● The system is easy to use. The card holds all the information necessary for automatic configuration and log-on.
● Context-sensitive help facilities can be provided, where appropriate, in the knowledge that they will only be seen by authorised users.
● The card can be used as a portable and updatable personal data store.

Using the Viewdate information station

When the MFile station is switched on, it displays a welcome message.

To activate the station the cardholder must first place his card on the coupler. The terminal and card then interrogate each other using encrypted messages. If the terminal is satisfied that the card is valid and the card is satisfied that the terminal is valid, the cardholder will be asked to enter his PIN using the terminal's keyboard. Although the echoes of the keystrokes are shown as stars on the screen, the PIN is not recorded in the terminal but sent directly to the card for checking. If the card is not valid, or if the cardholder has three unsuccessful attempts at his PIN, the screen will display an appropriate message and the keyboard will remain locked.

After a successful verification the cardholder is offered a choice of three options on a menu:

- Check card status/transaction history.
- Change personal number.
- Access viewdata system.

The card status check enables a cardholder to view the card's last 64 transactions, and the cardholder can choose to view MCash or MTill transactions separately. As well as showing the amount, the screen will also show the date, time and location of a purchase. The workstation can also give an analysis of transactions by pre-selected categories, such as food, books, bar, sports, etc. In addition, the cardholder is given basic information including the last time MCash was loaded and the amount of credit remaining in the card.

As the memory capacity of the card is limited, the terminal stores the foreground information, or template, and only the cardholder's individual records are retrieved from the card.

The way in which the PIN can be changed is quite simple. The cardholder has to enter the old number, then enter the new number twice. The card and terminal communicate with each other and the cardholder's PIN is changed.

If the cardholder has chosen to use one of the viewdata services, the terminal interrogates the card to see how much MCash is stored in it. As charges for the services are deducted automatically the terminal has to be sure that there is a pre-set minimum, in this case £1, in the card. Following that check, the cardholder indicates which viewdata service number is to be dialled. For added security the card, not the terminal, contains the telephone numbers. When the database responds, the terminal deducts MCash from the card. Charges are time based and are set by the Midland Bank as the provider of the service to recover only the price charged by Prestel. The top line of the display shows:

- The amount of charges incurred so far – this increases with every minute of use.
- The amount of MCash left in the card.

The user is warned of any special page charges about to be incurred by a brief message on the screen.

Another choice on the viewdata menu is the Thomas Cook Travel Information Service. Students can read information about foreign countries as well as the British Rail timetables. Through a third service, Thomas Cook Travel Money, it is also possible to order foreign currency and travellers' cheques which are paid for – though not with the smart card – on collection from the bank a couple of days later.

A printout of any list of transactions stored on the card, or any viewdata screen, can be obtained at two of the three MFile locations.

There is a supervisor's card, used at the MFile station, which has more memory and gives access to a different main menu. It is used to set the date, time, and the time charges for each database – these can be different during peak and off-peak times. The supervisor is the only person who can see or change these charges. The supervisor's card gives access to an audit trail which records key information relating to the use of the supervisor's cards and their access to the terminal.

Costs and benefits

Retailers benefit in many ways from the smart card system:

- Transactions are shorter and they can move people through till check-outs (EFTPOS units in this case) more quickly.
- They no longer need to spend time comparing the signature on the cheque with the signature on the card.
- The till itself checks the hot card file so that there is no need to look through lists of numbers on paper.
- The day's takings are more secure, held electronically in an EFTPOS unit or a smart card than they are in notes and coins.

The benefits to the cardholder reflect those to the retailer:

- As transactions take less time at the till, shopping is quicker and easier.
- There are no cheques to write.

- The card is more secure than existing bank cards. The use of the PIN ensures that no one but the cardholder can use the card for transactions larger than £20. The hot card file helps to prevent a lost or stolen card from being used.
- It is easy to keep track of spending by viewing transactions at the MFile station.
- The cardholder does not necessarily have to go to the bank to load MCash.
- The cardholder has access to Prestel and the Thomas Cook Travel Service.

The bank benefits, too, from smart card use:

- There is a reduction in processing costs. The cost of processing a cheque can be as much as 60p.
- The increased security of the card makes fraud less likely and this is an important factor.
- Added services, such as Prestel in this trial, could encourage more customers to use the bank.

The smart card is a fairly expensive item in comparison with an ordinary card. However, the smart card can last up to three times as long and this is important as the cost of issuing a card is relatively high. The cost per year of a smart card, in comparison with an ordinary card, is very favourable when issuing costs are taken into consideration.

Extension of the trial

The experiment at Loughborough was originally set to run for the academic year 1988/89, ending in July. However, it has been so successful that the trial is to be extended for a minimum period of a further year with a number of new facilities added.

NORWAY – THE LILLESTRØM EXPERIMENT

The smart card experiment in the town of Lillestrøm was initially promoted by three institutions: Bergen Bank, the third largest commercial bank in Norway; Integrert Databehandling A/S (IDA) which is a computer service bureau for 80% of commercial banking in Norway; and the Norwegian Telecommunications Administration. Their intention was to run a pilot project in a representative town with a view to implementing smart card payment systems for shops and telephones nationwide. This small group was soon joined by the Norwegian Postal Administration and the two largest commercial banks, and three savings banks also participated.

The town of Lillestrøm was chosen for several reasons: it was relatively near Oslo, only 20km, making it easier for participants based in the capital to provide adequate support for the project; there was a reasonable concentration of shops; and the majority of potential card users would be residents of the town.

Technically, the project was based on the Blois experiment in France, with some alterations to suit the Norwegian environment. As financial resources were limited the alterations had to be minimal but this approach had the advantage of achieving a fairly short set-up time of 10 months. A later experiment, based on the Lillestrøm system, which took place in Bormio, Italy, was set up in four months.

The Lillestrøm project emphasised the need for understanding and co-operation between all parties. The project leader was recruited from IDA but he did not represent his company on the project's steering committee. Considerable efforts were made to ensure that all viewpoints were represented on the steering committee at a fairly high level. This not only helped to resolve potential conflicts of interest but provided all parties with insight into the many aspects of a payment system. An additional benefit of these discussions was to give the organisations involved a solid background for later negotiations.

The organisations represented included: the Norwegian Federation of Retailers; The Consumers' Association; the Shop Employees' Union, bank, post and telecom employees; managers of local supermarkets; and the participating banks. Members of staff from all these organisations were involved in various working groups and care was taken, from the start, to achieve a good working relationship between the retailers and the financial institutions.

The financial terms for participating in the scheme were as follows:

- Customers, free of charge.
- Retailers, a symbolic one-time charge of kr.2,000.
- Funding – divided between the major partners: IDA, the Telecom Administration and the Post Office.
- Marketing expenses – the major partners and the banks.
- Operating costs – IDA, the Telecom Administration and the financial institutions.

This simplified method of funding the scheme was used so that the experiment could be set up quickly. If more realistic terms had been calculated, negotiations would have delayed the start of the experiment. It was explicitly stated in the customers' contracts that the issue and use of a card would be free for the duration of the experiment, with the implication that they might not be in the future.

There were four types of card used in the experiment:

- The customer's Telebank card, for use in shops and payphones, which contained software for secure remote banking operations.
- The retailer's Telebank card which, in conjunction with a PIN, allowed a point-of-sale terminal to be opened and closed. This card enabled the retailer's account to be credited and provided the centre's phone number for transaction delivery. A retailer could have several cards so that batches of transactions could be sent and credited at different banks if required. This was found to be an important feature as it allowed retailers to retain their freedom of bank affiliation if they wanted.
- The bank employee's Telebank card to open and close the banking machines and allow confidential operations with a customer card to take place in a secure way.
- The prepaid Telecard which was sold at banks, shops, railway stations and post offices and could only be used in payphones.

Customers were not selected by the banks to participate in the experiment. Instead, all holders of bank or postal accounts were invited to apply for one of the 5,000 cards available. The start of the operation was publicly announced in August and a letter of invitation was sent to the 19,000 account holders. A surprising 3,700 positive replies were received during the first week. By Christmas, all the point-of-sale terminals were installed, 15 payphones were operational, the banks had their support equipment and the last of the 5,000 ordered cards had been delivered to the banks. Also in December, 5,000 Telecards went on sale.

The point-of-sale terminals were installed as follows:

- 19 in groceries and supermarkets.
- 10 in clothing shops.
- 1 at the state wine and liquor monopoly.
- 2 in post offices.
- 5 at petrol stations.

In addition, 15 payphones accepted both the Telebank Card and the pre-paid Telecard.

Each financial establishment was equipped with a banking machine and an enquiry machine. The banking machine's main purpose was to allow change of the PIN code (once per card), change of the purchase power and to unblock cards with PIN code errors. These operations were recorded in a cartridge in the terminal which also contained a hot card list. The machine had a second card reader as some operations required the presence of both the bank employee's card and the customer's card. This machine was polled by the central collection and distribution system in the same way as the point-of-sale terminals.

The enquiry machine enabled a customer, using the PIN code, to check some of the contents of the card, such as purchase power, the current month's transactions or all transactions since the card was issued. This information was provided, on a self-service basis, on a small videotext screen and could be printed whenever the customer wished. In addition, it was possible to see, on the screen, the number of telephone units purchased and available. This type of equipment was stand-alone. All the terminals were provided by Bull which also made the Telebank Card incorporating a monochip microcomputer.

The point-of-sale terminal was a stand-alone version which required the purchase total to be keyed in. It had a battery-backed cartridge where transactions and a hot card list were stored. A modem and automatic dialling system provided the communications link with the clearing centre. The retailer could initiate a call to the clearing centre but, more usually, the machine was called automatically at night to collect the day's transactions and to deliver an updated hot card list. The customer's PIN code was checked in the card. Checking of the validity date, purchase power and hot card list were done by the terminal. After three PIN code errors the card was blocked completely and could only be unblocked by the issuing bank. Cards on the hot list were immediately and permanently locked out.

The automatic collection of transactions from point-of-sale terminals, and the delivery of the hot card list, was controlled by a central microcomputer produced by Sligos. The automatic dialling system was provided by Thomson-TITN. This collection operation took place between 19.30 and 20.30 every evening for 50 machines. The data was saved on floppy discs and exchanged with the clearing host.

A problem that frequently occurred was that attempts to call point-of-sale terminals automatically did not get through due to congestion in the telephone network. Retailers then had to make calls themselves the following morning. A fully digital telephone exchange, which is being installed in Lillestrøm, should improve the situation.

The payphones accepted two types of cards as stated previously: a pre-paid card, with 15 or 40 units (the Telecard), and the Telebank card, which required the PIN code, for purchasing 40 units and using them. Additional units could be purchased during a phone call as soon as a threshold was reached and without interrupting an on-going conversation.

At the end of the experiment about 140,000 transactions, having a total value of 34 m kroner, had been carried out with the Telebank card. The monthly figures gradually built up to around 9,500 transactions, as shown in Fig. 8.7, having a value of 2m kroner, but decreasing towards the end of the experiment. Of the 5,000 cards offered, 4,700 were collected by customers and 3,800 people used them. About 500 holders of the Telebank card had purchased telephone units. A total of 32,195 units were purchased in the first six months using both the Telebank cards and Telecards.

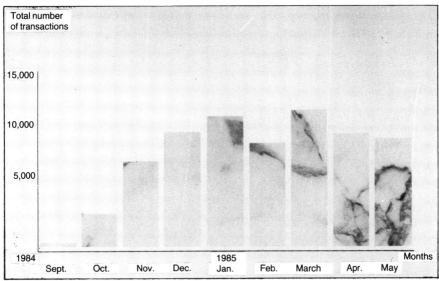

Fig. 8.7. Changes in number of payment transactions per month during the Lillestrøm experiment

Smart cards were most often used in grocery stores where 75% of the total number of transactions took place. The customers' attitudes were largely, very positive. An earlier enquiry had shown that people were in favour of the system being expanded and of having more functions available on the card. This is a particularly strong point for the smart card, especially as it has such effective security. The majority of users were aged between 35 and 45 years, not young people as had originally been expected.

Many people were surprised that 92% of the transactions were for amounts of less than 500 kroner and 98% were for less than 2,500 kroner, which is the check guarantee limit in Norway. This had a considerable effect on later decisions that were taken, particularly in relation to operations and communications costs.

The Norwegian Federation of Retailers has publicly stated that a retailer should not be burdened with communications costs. Initially, the retailers' position was that they should not have to pay for terminals either. This attitude was understandable at a stage when they were not sufficiently convinced of the advantages of electronic payment. A survey conducted at the end of the trial period, showed that retailers were, on the whole, pleased with the way the experiment had gone and felt that their customers were too. There were, however, some areas where they and their employees were not entirely satisfied and these were largely concerned with the equipment. The main causes of irritation were the telephone network, location of the terminal, problems due to the power supply, first generation cumbersome equipment and lack of maintenance during the weekends.

When asked about the possibility of being connected to a nation-wide system, the majority of retailers were interested but concerned about the costs involved. They seemed to be prepared to consider paying for terminals if there were many more customers using the card and if the costs were lower than the suggested figure of 5,000 kroner.

Surveys and analyses have shown that investment in this type of system will prove profitable for larger shops in Norway. If 20% of transactions were paid for by card, an off-line system would provide cost savings to shops with a turnover of above 8m kroner per year.

Half-way through the experiment the different partners discussed the possibility of continuing after 31 March 1986 but they decided after some hesitation, to discontinue the project as planned. However, during this time the Norwegian Federation of Retailers and the Norwegian Commercial Banks' Association signed a declaration of intent to introduce an electronic payment system using both smart cards and magnetic stripe technology with the capability of working off-line. This did not exclude the possibility of some authorisation operations being conducted in real time.

The resulting agreement confirmed the intention of the parties involved to co-operate during the introduction of the new system and it established the contributions to costs that each partner would be required to make. This agreement, between banks and retailers, may well be the first of its kind in the world. The Norwegian Bankers'

Association decided to make the smart card its primary method of payment by EFTPOS in Norway and a new project began in Lillestrøm in 1986.

9 MEDICAL APPLICATIONS

A S BETTER health care and longer life expectancy result in an increasingly geriatric society, the cost of maintaining medical care will continue to rise steadily. Added to this is the problem of keeping track of the expanding volume of medical records. In many countries the administrative system for health services is already stretched. Applications of the smart card in this area can help to cut down costs and improve efficiency while, at the same time, providing real benefits to patients, doctors and pharmacists. There are a number of possible applications in the medical field where smart cards can be applied and some are described in the following sections.

SOME PRINCIPAL USES

GENERAL MEDICAL CARD

As a general medical card the smart card could contain information such as:

- Holder's address, date of birth and next of kin.
- Name and address of doctor.
- Recent medical history.
- Serious complaints.
- Allergies.
- Drugs being taken.
- Donor wishes.

The card could be carried by the individual and in the event of an emergency, such as the holder collapsing in the street, it could provide

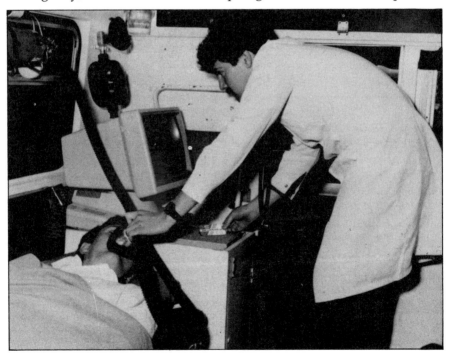

Fig. 9.1. A smart card could provide vital medical information to an ambulance crew or doctor at the scene of an accident. (Photograph courtesy of GEC)

immediate information to an ambulance crew or doctor (see Fig. 9.1). The speed with which vital information could be available may well save lives.

The cost to a health organisation of implementing such a scheme could well be relatively small as many people would see the card as a form of insurance and be prepared to pay for it themselves.

The smart card could hold information concerning the patient's recent medical history, say for the previous six months, which, in many cases, would be all the information a doctor would require. If the patient carried the card to his appointment it would not be necessary for the doctor to have the patient's file in front of him. At the end of the consultation the doctor's notes could be recorded on the card and a copy printed out for the file. At present, on occasions, a great amount of effort has to be put into locating a patient's records and getting them to the right place at the right time. If each patient was issued with a smart card the paper records could be kept for reference only and for use if a card is lost. A smart card system could prove to be cheaper than installing, say, a computer network in a large hospital for location and retrieval of patients' records.

A smart card medical record could prove useful to doctors and district nurses caring for patients discharged early from hospital. At present it can be several days before a doctor or district nurse receives the patient's notes and this can cause delay in giving the patient correct treatment. If the patient's notes could be accessed by the health professionals, from a smart card through a portable card reader, administrative procedures could be improved.

The smart card does not, as yet, have enough memory capacity to store a patient's complete medical history, especially, for example, when it comes to storing a digitised X-ray picture.

DRUG ISSUE CARD

This card could be most useful to patients receiving regular medication. Some old people, for instance, take as many as 12 different drugs at a time. At present the patient has to fill in forms and get the doctor's authorisation for each repeat prescription. This is time consuming and wasteful. The drug issue card could contain the amounts to be prescribed and the frequency with which they should be dispensed. It would facilitate accurate control over the drugs issued to an individual, ensuring that no more than a certain amount was prescribed in a given period. In particular, the card could be useful in controlling the issue of dangerous drugs.

A drug issue card could replace written prescriptions if doctors were required to record the prescriptions in the card instead of on paper. This would have the advantage of eliminating the risk of the pharmacist misinterpreting the doctor's handwriting and could also save time for the pharmacist if the card were able to initiate automatic label printing.

A drug issue card would be useful to dentists, providing information not currently at their disposal about medication prescribed to the patient. The flow of information could move both ways, telling the doctor of any drugs prescribed during dental treatment.

DIABETIC CARD

Diabetes affects between 1% and 2% of the population. In the UK nearly one million people suffer from this condition and approximately half of these attend a hospital diabetic clinic once a week with many seeing the doctor on a regular basis. With an increasing emphasis on shared care, a patient might be attending as many as five specialist diabetes services at any one time as well as consulting with a specialist, nurse and family doctor.

The present system has numerous sets of records being held independently. A vast amount of correspondence is required if adequate communication is to be maintained between all the people involved in the care of a patient. The smart card can help solve this problem by providing a personalised data store that can be carried by the patient from one clinic to the next. The card gives a complete view of the patient's progress, which does not exist under the present system, and ensures that up-to-date records are available to all concerned. Each specialist would still keep his own paper records and, in the event of a patient losing his card, the information could be retrieved from these. In the same way, the smart card would also be an ideal portable record medium for patients undergoing regular dialysis treatment.

ANTE-NATAL CARD

Ante-natal care in the UK is often shared between the hospital ante-natal clinic, the expectant mother's own doctor and the community midwife. It is important that there is adequate communication between these parties, ensuring that they all have access to up-to-date records. As the expectant mother moves from one place to another for her ante-natal care, a brief summary of each visit could be recorded on the card so that details of her blood pressure, weight and general condition are always readily available.

One barrier to effective communication that could be eliminated by a smart card would be the doctor's handwriting. In some cases the summary written on the patient's record card is illegible to a different doctor at the next visit. The smart card could contain a complete record of the patient's ante-natal care and could save time spent in locating the expectant mother's notes at hospital ante-natal clinics. At the time of birth the records would be available immediately. Afterwards data stored on the card could be printed out for permanent storage and, with some smart cards, the memory could be erased so that the card could be reissued to another person.

STAFF IDENTIFIER

The card is an ideal method by which entry to a hospital can be controlled, particularly at night when many small hospitals lock their doors. The smart card could also control access to areas where medical records are kept, pharmacies and departments where there are potentially dangerous machines such as X-ray equipment. It could also be used as a staff time card.

SOME INTERNATIONAL EXAMPLES

In FRANCE, an electronic data acquisition system, known as SESAM, has been adopted by the French social security to assist with the administration of illness insurance.

The illness insurance scheme allows a person to choose his own general practitioner, dentist, pharmacist or specialist and to go to the hospital of his choice whether public or private. The patient must, however, pay the fees himself in the first instance. A claim is then submitted to the social security system and part or all of the fees will be reimbursed. There are 129 regional illness insurance districts (CPAM) which are connected by a computer network to 33 computer centres. These centres deal with large computer data processing. Each CPAM is equipped with dedicated computers for processing all data necessary for the refund of patients' fees.

The aim of the SESAM system is to improve data acquisition using advanced technology. The management of the local refunding system in the regional offices could then be improved and the health form eliminated. This would have several advantages: the number of archival forms which need to be kept would be limited; more information about the consumption of medical services would be available; and the medical professionals would have more time to spend on their patients.

SESAM is based on the idea of using a smart card to replace the paper card issued by the regional offices. The card chosen was the Bull CP8 card with 8kbits of EPROM memory.

The patient's card contains only administrative data records. However, the medical practitioner also has a smart card which enables him to access the information held on the patient's card as well as containing professional identification and information for social security administration.

The system includes a small, portable data acquisition system which records details of patients' medical care and fees along with administrative information held on both the patients' and medical practitioners' cards. The small, portable terminal allows the practitioner to work all day without either recharging or reloading the batteries – which is particularly useful during home visits.

A separate transmission device is installed in the practitioner's office and, in the evening, it is connected to the portable terminal containing the day's data. During the night an automatic data transmission system, which is set up in the regional illness insurance offices, calls all the transmission devices and collects the day's data using an automatic dial unit.

The pharmacist uses a personal computer with two card readers and software installed by the national illness insurance office. These enable him to read the patient's details, recorded on the card, and dispense the correct medication. In the evening the pharmacist transmits all the data stored during the day to the regional illness insurance offices. In 1984 and 1985 six regional offices were chosen for trials of the SESAM system. The aims of the first phase were to evaluate:

- The relationships between the different parties involved in the system.
- The patients' acceptance of the card.
- The acceptability of the system to the practice and pharmacy.
- Additionally, the first phase was intended to promote a better knowledge and acceptance of the system among medical practition-

ers not involved in the trial and, more generally, to assess the viability of the scheme.

The pilot trials were held in five places: Blois, Charleville, Mezieres, Evreaux, Lens and Rennes. Every pilot site consisted of a limited geographical area with a fairly small number of families and pharmacists – about 3,000–5,000 people and 3–5 pharmacists.

Experiments have also been carried out in France using smart cards as health cards, recording patients' medical information and treatment (see Fig. 9.2). This is a different application from the health insurance cards which were intended only for administrative purposes. The smart card has two main features which make it suitable for use in the health sector: security and data storage.

The health cards in the experiments can be used as a portable medical file, carried by the patient, which can be read and written to by doctors consulted. To read the patient's card the doctor must insert

Fig. 9.2. Smart cards are used as health cards in France and other countries. (Photograph courtesy of Bull)

both his own access card and the patient's card into a reader which is connected either to a Minitel – the national videotext terminal – or to a computer. The information can be printed by an on-line printer if required. A pilot trial of these health cards, known as Carte Sante, began in 1985 in Blois. In this initial trial the cards were used as a tool for communication between doctors. Groups of people who made frequent use of the preventative or curative system, and who were likely to change doctors were identified. The groups selected were pregnant women, infants up to two years and people over 65 years.

Since 1985 the cards have been available to pregnant women and children born in Blois. All doctors in Blois have been offered Minitels and related readers. The experiment with people aged over 65 years aims to provide information for initial consultations with new doctors and emergency situations. The doctor enters on the card the main diseases, allergies and prostheses and can update major treatment data seven times. Entries concerning blood values can only be made by laboratory biologists.

Another experiment, taking place in northern France, involves Lille University helping a medical society to design the software of a card called 'Biocarte'. This, chiefly, works in ambulatory care. The equipment needed to read the cards has to be specially fitted to the emergency vehicle and can be a Minitel or a microcomputer, or a portable reader made by Logicam.

A smart card, named Santal, is being used in an experiment which is being run in the St. Nazaire area. This card has been offered to around 30,000 hospital and clinical patients from eight public and private hospitals and is intended to provide information for the doctors while improving administrative procedures.

The trials have, so far, shown that patients see the positive uses of the card. They see it as a document, describing their state of health, which they keep themselves and can hand over to a doctor of their choice – being 'on the computer' does not seem to worry them. Their interests are protected by the Commission Nationale de l'Informatique et des Libertés. In one of the experiments, Biocarte, the patients pay for the card.

Evaluation of the trials is continuing because it is important for the Directorate of Health to know how cost-effective the cards are before extending the system to cover larger areas of the country.

In the UNITED KINGDOM there is a trial under way using smart cards to carry medical records. The experiment is taking place in Exmouth in Devon where 9,000 smart cards, known as Care Cards, have been issued to patients. The patients chosen to take part in the scheme included:

- All the patients of one small group practice.
- All people aged under five and over sixty-five years within a large group practice.
- All diabetics in Exmouth.

The equipment to read and write to the cards was made available at both group practices, Exmouth hospital, Exeter main hospital (Wonford), a large dental practice in Exmouth and all pharmacies in Exmouth. Medical information was entered into the card at the beginning of the trial by the patient's doctor and the patient is now able to present the card each time he visits a health professional. Patients are able to view information held on the cards on terminals in practices participating in the scheme. If a card becomes full or is lost it can be reissued by the patient's doctor. The trial will continue until 1990.

The health professionals have to use a key card to access the patient information in the Care Card and both patients and professionals have a PIN for extra security. Different levels of access are allowed and these are determined by codes within the card. Doctors, for example, have access to all the information in the card whereas other professionals, such as pharmacists, have limited access.

In the UNITED STATES, smart cards are being used in several medical applications. Personal Health Card Systems has implemented a scheme which uses a Micro Card Technology CP8 card to carry medical information. The cards have a multi-level, secure access system to enable confidential information to be protected and to ensure that only certain authorised people can update the information.

A doctor in California has set up a system which uses smart cards to carry emergency medical data such as allergies, current medications and current diagnoses. The emergency smart card works with his existing computerised medical records system which automatically extracts a summary of the patient's medical information to be directly entered into the smart card. This particular system does not require any skill to operate as, once the card is inserted into the reader, the information is shown automatically. However, a second card, which is held by the doctor, has to be inserted before confidential information can be viewed. The doctor using this system sees it as a way for hospitals to attract patients and encourage their loyalty.

Smart Card International, with InfoMed, is producing a smart card based scheme for home health care applications. The company will use the Ulticard which has its own integrated keyboard and display. It is hoped that the smart card will help to improve the efficiency of nurses making home visits. The nurse will enter an assessment of the patient's condition in the card and this information can be downloaded to the home-care agency later to calculate the costs to the patient. A card will also be held by the patient.

At the Florida hospital, in Orlando, the AT&T contactless smart card is involved in a six-month trial, recording medical data on patients undergoing extensive courses of treatment.

In JAPAN there are a number of trials of medical smart cards. One trial involves using a smart card to hold information relating to medical examinations. Over 40 categories of information can be stored on the card including the cardholder's identity, health insurance details, allergies and blood test results. The card is being carried by about 1,500 people and about 50 hospitals and other medical organisations are co-operating in the scheme.

In another trial the Seibu Saison Group distributed 12,000 smart cards in January 1986, for use as personal health records at 45 hospitals.

The Japanese Ministry of Welfare has also been studying the feasibility of introducing a national health card programme.

CASE STUDY

MEDICATION RECORD TRIALS IN WALES

This case study has been drawn from information supplied by Dr. Robert Stevens of the Welsh School of Pharmacy, University of Wales.

Trials, involving portable medication data records, have been run by a research group of the Welsh School of Pharmacy. The research group was seeking a way of creating individual medication records which would include medicines bought over the counter as well as those prescribed by a doctor. The intention was to build up a more complete record of drugs taken by the patient. Such records are now considered by pharmacists to be essential to good practice, enabling the pharmacist to check for adverse drug reactions between new and existing treatments and to offer the best advice when counselling patients. This type of record could be particularly useful for elderly patients who often have to take a number of different medicines and who regularly visit the same pharmacy.

Difficulties arise when attempting to maintain accurate records for patients using more than one pharmacy. As a result, most pharmacies do not have drug records, even for regular patients, and rely on the pharmacist's memory of the patient's history when checking a new therapy. Patients unknown to the pharmacist have to be interviewed, which is an unreliable and time-wasting method of obtaining the required information. Trials, with disk-based computerised record systems, led to the conclusion that some form of computerised record was essential. The record produced, however, would almost certainly be incomplete and did not justify the expense of a computer which incorporated disk storage.

The drug information held in the doctor's records was decided upon as the source of information for the record. A way had to be found, however, of obtaining that information without breaching confidentiality. Network systems were dismissed on the grounds of cost, security and speed of data transfer. The answer was to provide the patient with an abstract of the medication record in a form accessible to a computer, which could be read and updated at each visit to the doctor or pharmacy.

This approach fitted in with the traditional structure of the British National Health Service in which the doctor (GP) holds the patient's medical records and is the patient's primary contact with the health service. Data added to the portable record could also be retained on a master surgery record which remained under the ultimate control of the GP.

System concepts

The first step in designing a patient retained record system was the selection of a suitable device to hold the record. Interest in the form of the portable record now centres on smart cards and optical technology. In 1983 the choices were more limited.

Experience with trials of paper records carried by the patient had shown that the novelty soon wore off and patients began to forget to bring the record with them when visiting the pharmacy. The ideal device, therefore, had to be one which would be carried automatically by the patient, at all times outside the home, and which could withstand a considerable amount of wear and tear. The nature of the data to be stored in the device suggested that a reprogrammable memory would be best suited to the experiment and a device containing an EEPROM was sought.

Cost was considered an important factor for the successful implementation of the system and the cost of both the device and the read/write system was considered carefully. A survey of community pharmacies in the UK had shown clearly that £1,500 was the maximum acceptable price for the computer, printer and card reader.

The cards available at that time possessed PROM memories of low capacity and their physical robustness in every day use was largely unproven. The device chosen for the system came from Datakey as it met at least some if not all of the requirements. It was in the shape of a key, very rugged, contained an EEPROM (although of very limited capacity) and it was hoped that patients would carry it attached to their domestic key-rings. The system was called MEDLOCK.

Phase 1

By the spring of 1984 a prototype, fixed site unit had been developed which comprised:

- A host microcomputer (a Lynx 48k model) and visual display unit (VDU).
- A custom-built interface unit.
- A Keytroller.
- A Keyceptacle.

The Keyceptacle was a socket into which the key was inserted. It provided a passive connection between the token and the Keytroller. The Keytroller managed the passage of data between the key and the host microcomputer, controlling all input and output operations. The data token keys possessed 240 bytes of usable memory.

The limited size of this memory restricted the use of the prototype but the system was installed in a pharmacy in May 1984. The key was programmed to accept a record which consisted of patient identifier information, a record of four dispensed drugs and details of repeat prescriptions.

Phase 1 of the trial was partly sponsored by the Pharmaceutical Society of Great Britain and lasted for one year. It involved the selection of 50 patients by the pharmacist and was restricted to people regularly using four or less drugs.

There were three main reasons for installing the prototype:

- To gauge patient acceptance of such a record and the willingness of the patient to return the key with a repeat prescription.
- To assess staff acceptance of the system.
- To provide a practical test-bed for software developments.

Several factors which emerge from that early trial determined the course of future work.

- The speed of data access was critical if the system was to be acceptable in a real environment. The Datakey prototype read and displayed the stored information in approximately 30 seconds and that was unacceptably slow.
- Tokens used in a busy environment require an external patient identifier. At times confusion occurred when several keys were handed in at the same time.
- Although attaching the key to a key-ring ensured its return to the patient, some people were reluctant to hand the key-ring over to pharmacy staff. Attempts to remove the key from the ring slowed down prescription processing.
- The EEPROM was ideal for the types of data being processed, but a minimum of 1.5kbyte of EEPROM, or an even greater capacity PROM chip, were essential for a full medication record.
- The cost of the token had to be drastically reduced.

Two major issues were resolved by the trial. Staff acceptance of the concept was good and many of their suggestions were incorporated in future phases. None of the 50 patients approached refused to take part and 70% of the keys were regularly returned. The Datakey proved to be a strong token and only one unit failed in the course of the 12-month trial.

Phase 2

Phase 2 of the trial involved replacement of the Datakey by an alternative device, expansion of the software and replacement of the Lynx computer by a more powerful computer. The new token chosen took the form of a 16kbyte PROM card supplied by the MIPS Corporation of Japan. The new computer chosen was the Sinclair QL, a more sophisticated microcomputer at lower cost. Additional hardware had to be constructed to allow the cards to be read and written to by the computer.

A six-month, pharmacy-only trial of the card, hardware and new software completed Phase 2 of the trial. The performance of the 100 cards issued was good with no failures being reported. Patients were again willing to accept the cards but the return rate fell to 50%. The expanded memory capacity permitted a full drug record to be kept and pharmacy staff began to see the full potential of the system.

Several conclusions were drawn at the end of Phase 2:

- The card could be a suitable medium for storing the record.
- Speed of access had to be improved.
- Doctor participation in the trial was essential to ensure return of the cards with the prescriptions.

Phase 3

In Phase 3, consideration was given to the expansion of the system to include the participation of doctors. The intention was to provide doctors with portable card readers and computers which would enable them to have access to the medication data during home visits. As a result, three different types of terminals were assembled for Phase 3. These were:

- A fixed site terminal capable of reading and modifying the record for the pharmacist. The simplest equipment configuration was required in the pharmacy, where no permanent storage of information was to occur. All data would be stored in the card presented by the patient. The equipment used in the pharmacy consisted of a Sinclair QL with an extended 640kbyte RAM, a card read/write unit, a printer and a VDU.
- A fixed site terminal, capable of reading and modifying the record, with data storage in the form of a hard disk, for keeping a master record in the surgery. That system comprised a CST Thor computer with an integral 20Mbyte (20,000kbytes) Winchester hard disk and single floppy disk drive, a read/write unit, a printer and a VDU.
- A portable terminal, for doctors on domiciliary visits, consisting of a Dulmont portable computer, a card reader and a portable printer.

A read/write unit was developed and this interfaced directly with the databus of the QL or Thor computer, providing the required reading and writing speed. The new read/write unit was capable of transferring 4kbyte from the card to the computer in 0.5 seconds, giving virtually instantaneous access to data.

Phase 3 involved the issue of some 2,500 cards to patients registered with one GP practice. Copies of the information held on the cards were kept on the hard disk in the surgery. The system performed the following functions:

- Record a 'page' of personal identification details and information useful to both the pharmacist and GP (see Fig. 9.3).

Name: Smith Mary **Sex:** F **Blood group:** AB+ **Marital status:** M				
Address: 15 Station Road, Anytown, Glam CF9 40I. Phone: (0222) 123456				
NHS: XYZ 23456	**NI:** 123456	**Birthdate:** 130156		
FP1001: 121286	**TET:** 010385	**Smear:**150684		
Chronic: Asthma Bronchitis Diabetes	**Donor:** Kidney Eye			
Allergies: Aspirin Penicillin				
Next of kin: Smith John 77 Fishers Cottage Windsor, Berkshire PP9 8FF **Phone:** (01555) 5874	**Doctor:** Dr. Williams **Phone:** (0222) 987543 **Comments:** Insulin dependent diabetic			

Fig. 9. 3. Patient identification page – Welsh medication trials. (Note: NHS – National Health Service number; NI – National Insurance number)

- Record drug items prescribed to the patient and indicate, on the card, the number of times each has been repeated (see Fig. 9.4).
- Automatically prepare prescriptions by using data indicated on the card.
- Check for adverse drug interactions between drugs, the names of which, are stored on the card and the new prescription being entered.
- Provide the pharmacist with a means of endorsing the prescription at the time of dispensing and automatically add to the record the number of days between prescribing and dispensing.
- Automatically prepare drug labels using data stored on the card.
- Issue new or replacement cards using data stored on the hard disk.
- Transfer data to the hard disk from the card. At each surgery consultation the card could be used to access the master surgery record through an identification code. The master record was compared with the data on the card and automatic updating performed.

Date	Drug	FO	Str	Qty	Instr	Repeat	Disp	L
120386/	Aspirin	ta	300MG	30	1-2/8H/WW/PC		2	1
230486/	Aspirin	ta	300MG	30	1-2/8H/WW/PC	120386	1	2
210586/	Aspirin	ta	300MG	30	1-2/8H/WW/PC	230486		3

Fig. 9.4. Drug information page – Welsh medication trials.

The MEDLOCK medical record system was designed to be quick and easy to operate. Help instructions are displayed on the screen at all times, either in the form of menus at the bottom of the screen or as specific instructions. Staff training proved trouble-free with an overall average of one hour's instruction being quite sufficient. Fig. 9.3 shows the information displayed when a card is first accepted by the system.

Patient identification information followed a fairly standard pattern. Supplementary information, relevant to prescribing or to the purchase of drugs by the patient, was also included on the first page in two specific categories:

- Chronic health conditions liable to influence the choice of drugs prescribed to the patient or purchased by the patient, e.g. diabetes or heart disease.
- Drugs to which the patient had demonstrated allergy or adverse reaction.
- Additional information, helpful to the GP in the everyday administration of patient care, was also included in the form of:
- Date of the last cervical smear.
- Date of an annual consultation relating to contraceptive advice (FP1001).
- Date of last immunisation booster (tetanus).
- Blood group.

Additional fields were included, to provide information relating to organ donors, plus a comments field to permit the doctor to add any supplementary comments which he felt necessary.

Fig. 9.4 illustrates the information included in the rest of the record which was a full list of medications prescribed or purchased by the patient. The table shows the format for the addition of three consecutive prescriptions for the same drug. Line 1 represents the first prescription for the item and lines 2 and 3 represent two subsequent repeats. The bold print represents a marker included in the program to indicate that the pharmacist has dispensed both lines 1 and 2. Line 1 was dispensed two days after prescribing and line 2 one day after prescribing. When using a colour monitor, dispensed lines were indicated by a green line number and lines awaiting dispensing indicated by a red line number. It can be seen from the table that the repeat column indicates the date of the previous prescription and the number of times that the drug has been repeated.

In previous trials the computerised production of labels for dispensed medicines on conventional hardware had been monitored.

Depending on the skill of the operator, between 5 and 10 seconds were required to enter the name of the patient. By extracting data from the card, patient's name, repeat drug names and instructions were automatically copied from selected fields in the record eliminating much typing and tedium.

A similar procedure was adopted for the preparation of repeat prescriptions in the surgery. If no changes to quantity or instructions were required, selection of a drug line and printing to the paper prescription form was reduced to three keystrokes.

Observations on Phase 3

On-site work commenced in May 1986 with the compilation of hard disk master records for 2,930 of the 4,500 patients registered with the practice at the trial surgery. The sample included all patients regularly receiving repeat medications (approximately 750) and a random selection from the remainder. Of the patients selected, the ratio of females to males was 1 : 12:1 and Fig. 9.5 provides an analysis, by age, of that initial sample.

Card issue started in October 1986 and continued until June 1987. Individual patients, or a representative from each family, were interviewed. They were asked to verify the authenticity of the data held on the master record and whether they objected either to carrying the card or to the data it contained. Budget and time constraints meant that a total of 2,500 cards were issued. Three patients refused to accept a card but one of them later changed her mind.

After verification, the data was transferred from the disk to the card and the card handed to the patient with an explanatory leaflet. Patients were asked to make sure that the card was returned to the surgery at each visit. Clearly, a more general issue of such cards would need to be carried out in a less time-consuming manner, but the exercise was partly aimed at patient education.

Installation of the equipment and staff training were performed in stages. The pharmacy presented little problem, all staff having been involved in previous trials. Similarly, acceptance by the surgery receptionists presented no real headaches. The system was very easy to use and minimal training was required to produce a relatively competent operator – both the receptionists and pharmacy used the system live from the first day of card issue.

The doctors presented more of a problem and their use of the system during consultations was deliberately delayed until March 1987, when it was anticipated that all the software and hardware bugs would have been removed. None of the doctors were computer literate and there

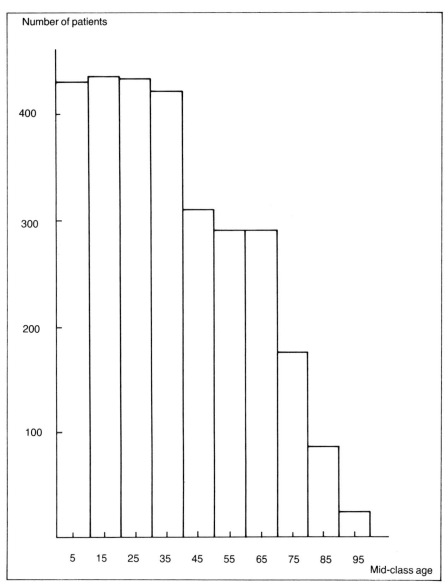

Fig. 9.5 Age distribution of patient sample selected – Welsh medication trials.

was a genuine fear that operation of the system would disrupt doctor/patient communication.

Much thought was given to the best time and the best way in which doctor involvement would take place. Consideration was given to the following:

- Would system usage prove a feasible proposition during a very busy surgery? Although many surgeries use computers, few systems actually require the doctor to use a terminal during consultations.
- Would it slow down the processing of patients?
- Would all partners in the practice use it?
- Would patients object to the use of the system during consultations?

In the event, five of the doctors were willing to use the system, while one was not. It did, initially, slow down patient processing in the consulting room and in very busy surgeries it was sometimes not used for every patient. However, after familiarisation, the interruption was minimised and several software modifications are now in hand to further reduce delays. The major complaint from the doctors was that medication records alone did not fully exploit the potential of the system and that the inclusion of clinical data was urgently required. Delay was acceptable to the doctors if the benefits outweighed the inconvenience.

The provision of a portable terminal for use during domiciliary visits was perceived as one of the greatest advantages of card records.

Approximately one year after installation the activities of patients attending the surgery were monitored. A record was kept of the purpose of each patient visit to the surgery and Fig. 9.6 provides a comparison of patients attending for a consultation with those simply requiring a repeat prescription. An average of 39.7 patients per consultation period was recorded over a seven-week period, with 42% requiring repeat prescriptions. Repeat prescriptions are issued at any time during surgery hours.

When card usage of different age groups was compared it was found that patients over the age of 70 had the highest rate of utilisation. It had been anticipated that usage would reflect the more frequent need for medication among the elderly but it was encouraging to see that 85% of the older people in the trial were using the cards. A concern expressed at the beginning of the trial was that older patients would either not accept the system or would forget to bring the card with them. The initial results suggest that this was not the case.

A factor of considerable interest was the ability of the cards and read/write units to withstand repeated use. Reliability of the devices was 100% but quantification of the number of transactions performed by each device was difficult because no internal logging procedure was introduced. The heaviest use of the read/write units occurred in the

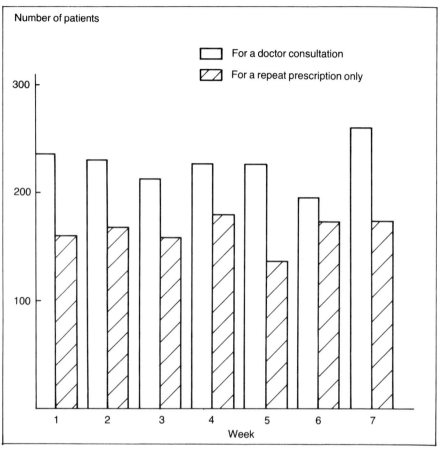

Fig. 9.6 Analysis of patients attending surgery – Welsh medication trials

pharmacy and in the surgery reception area.

Involvement of the surgery reduced the problem associated with earlier pharmacy-only trials by improving the return of the record. Patients quickly came to realise that repeat prescriptions were processed much more quickly if the card was presented at the surgery. With a majority of the prescriptions being dispensed directly after a visit to the surgery, the card was more often available to the pharmacist. At the surgery the number of patients failing to return their cards actually dropped over the trial period. This level of patient compliance suggests that surgery managed records of this type would provide a viable system for the majority of patients.

A total of 60.5% of the prescribed drug items recorded in the master hard disk record were endorsed to show that they had been dispensed in the trial pharmacy and carried a record of the number of days between prescribing and dispensing. Several factors could account for the lack of endorsement on the remaining lines. These are:

- Failure to present the card at the trial pharmacy.
- Items dispensed at a pharmacy not involved in the trial.
- Card not endorsed at the trial pharmacy.
- Completed card data not yet returned to the surgery master record (usually during a subsequent visit to the surgery).
- Item not dispensed.

No analysis has yet been performed to determine which of the above factors were significant.

In the pharmacy some frustrations were apparent. The software was designed primarily for use by pharmacists and dispensing technicians with a familiarity with drug labelling systems. The attempts to produce labelling instructions in the surgery did, on occasion, result in some bizarre patient instructions. Hence, the next version of the software will incorporate a modified labelling routine.

The Phase 3 system is still being used routinely to service the prescription needs of over 2,000 patients. For both the pharmacy and the surgery, MEDLOCK is now an accepted tool in the daily work routine.

Phase 4 (1987–. . .)

Work on the next phase has begun and is aimed at providing extended facilities to the user and an expanded record containing clinical data. The system will incorporate a contactless smart card developed by GEC Card Technology.

Thought is currently being given to the form which the record should take for further trials, to optimise the card's usefulness. Areas under consideration include:

- Extended patient identification data.
- Emergency medical record abstract.
- Full medication history.
- Significant laboratory data.
- Doctor's clinical summary.
- Message pad – to aid transfer of information from doctor to consultant and *vice versa*.

To ensure data compatibility with other systems available to the GP, both clinical and drug data will be coded.

10 LEISURE AND TRAVEL APPLICATIONS

SOME PRINCIPAL USES

LEISURE APPLICATIONS

WE ARE, undoubtedly, moving towards a society which will have more leisure time. With the resultant growth in the leisure industry the opportunities for smart cards to be applied in this area will grow considerably in the future.

The card could be used for allowing access to sports buildings, such as squash clubs, golf clubs and fitness centres. Units of time, number of games or electronic keys to items of fitness equipment could all be purchased and stored on the card. At the same time, the card could be used to record information about the performance and progress of the cardholder. The card could also be used for payments at sports club bars and restaurants.

The use of smart cards in leisure parks, such as Disneyland, and holiday complexes is another possibility. A number of units could be purchased and stored on the card when entering the park, then these could be used to 'buy' rides or turns on, say, the rifle range and slot machines, and so on. Winning points could even be stored on the card and could then be converted to prizes when the cardholder leaves the complex.

An important application for the card is likely to be as a ticket for large sporting events. For instance, a smart card could be used as a football supporter's identity card to control access to football grounds. The smart card could contain data such as the cardholder's identity, which football club he supports, match ticket and which part of the ground he has access to. The smart card could log the number of games attended and, after a pre-set number had been reached, the person could be given points for tickets to special games such as cup finals.

The Olympic Games is an important sporting event where serious consideration is being given to the use of smart cards. The card could act as a flexible ticket, giving access to different events, and could be used to pay for refreshments at the events. It would also be ideal as a very secure identity card issued to competitors at the games village.

As a season ticket for the opera, cinema and theatre, with incentives of, say, one free entry for the regular attendee, the smart card could be the ideal medium.

Smart cards could be issued to hotel guests for a variety of functions. A smart card could be used as a key to the door and the drinks cabinet in the room, or for recording meals taken and drinks ordered. When returned to the check-out point it could automatically calculate the bill for printing on a receipt.

Direct broadcasting by satellite (DBS) and cable television are already available in some countries and are going to become more widespread over the next few years. The smart card offers an ideal means for payment and reception of these services. Cards holding the key necessary to descramble the picture and decoding equipment could be purchased from television rental companies. After an interval of, for instance, one month, the key required could be changed so that the user has to return to the rental shop to pay to have the card updated. Viewing statistics could also be collected by the card and read when it is taken in for recharging. This would help television companies to tailor the programmes they produce to the types of programmes their viewers wish to watch.

TRAVEL APPLICATIONS

The smart card has great potential in the field of travel, making it possible for different functions to be combined on one card and simplifying procedures for the traveller.

Air travel, for example, could be made simpler using smart cards. The most enduring memory many people have of travelling by air is of crowds, queues and delays at the airport. Airlines attach great importance to the relationship between customer satisfaction and repeat business and it would be to their advantage to reduce, as far as possible, the level of stress experienced by the traveller. A smart card, issued to a passenger at the check-in desk, could combine various functions. The same card could, for instance, be used as a boarding pass and to control access to privilege facilities. If the card recorded which facilities were used it would be easier for the airport authority to monitor usage of facilities for market research and strategic planning purposes. When the boarding pass is handed in the information could easily be retrieved and, if the card was reprogrammable, it could be issued to another passenger.

Exchanging currency at an airport can be a headache for the traveller. A particular problem facing him is deciding how much foreign currency he will need in coin form for the various coin-operated services and vending machines in the airport concourse. This is experienced most by the long-haul traveller making brief stop-overs. It should be possible to reduce this problem if passengers can use one smart card, loaded with electronic credits at a bank, to operate all the machines and pay for services. The exchange process would be greatly simplified and commission charges might be reduced. This system would have benefits for the airport authority too as it would virtually eliminate coin-boxes as well as their associated maintenance costs and vulnerability to theft.

In the future, it is envisaged that there could be an electronic passport. The card could be placed in or on a reader in immigration control and could be validated by the holder using one of the personal identification techniques described in Chapter 7. This would not only speed up the process of immigration and visa checking but would make it far more difficult to forge passports.

Some types of smart cards could be issued as season travel tickets, which could also allow access through automatic ticket barriers. In Britain this would have important uses in data capture with the widespread deregulation of public transport. Information on subsidised and concessionary fares collected can be held securely on the card and this can be presented to the subsidising authority for payment.

SOME INTERNATIONAL EXAMPLES

Pathe Cinema in FRANCE has introduced a smart card as part of a wider marketing strategy designed to attract people back to the cinema. The Pathe card is pre-loaded with 10 tickets when it is purchased and when the customer presents it at the cinema the number of tickets required is debited from the card. The card can be reloaded seven times. The price of the card represents a considerable saving on buying 10 individual tickets.

Smart cards are being used by Club Méditerranée as keys to services and activities, (see Fig. 10.1). The cards will also replace beads as the accepted currency in club bars. For a test, in Marbella, a card is prepared in Paris for each guest and the cards and personal identification numbers are sent to the resort by courier. The cards can be used for purchases throughout the Marbella complex, even on the beach where transactions are stored in a portable off-line card reader. Videotext terminals around the complex enable guests to check their expenditures. The advantages of the card are that it reduces billing errors, is more convenient for the guest and allows Club Méditerranée to continue with its policy of eliminating the use of real money during club holidays. All accounts must, however, be settled before the

Fig. 10.1. Smart cards are being used by Club Méditerranée as keys to services and activities. (Photograph courtesy of Club Méditerranée)

guest's return air ticket is given back to him.

CP8 cards are in use, in the Biarritz region of France, to record information about golfer performance, and the French Disneyland near Paris, with its anticipated 50 million visitors each year, is expected to use smart cards for access to the park and hotel.

On-line lotteries have been in existence for some time in the UNITED STATES. In California the lottery involves the player choosing six out of 49 numbers. Fifteen million people are reported to have tried the lottery at least once and five million are regular players. Now, the lottery organisers are considering using smart cards instead of lottery tickets. The proposal is that a lottery terminal should be installed at a supermarket check-out. Up to 10,000 cards would be distributed to people interested in playing the game and customers could play an instant win/lose game while their shopping is being tabulated and packed.

In the Calgary and Seoul Olympic Games, France's 900 athletes were issued with smart cards containing administrative and medical data.

Satellite broadcasting involves the use of smart cards in JAPAN. To receive satellite television the viewer has to have a smart card to descramble the picture. The card also records the viewer's use of the service for the purpose of calculating fees.

In the UK, Sky Television Company is intending to use smart cards as decryption keys for satellite broadcasts. They have set up a company to manufacture low cost smart cards which will be replaced after three months' use. This is seen as the best way of ensuring the security of the system. The company expects to manufacture two million smart cards during the first year of introduction.

In the area of public transport in FRANCE, the smart card is being used as a ticket on the urban transport network in Blois, and the Societe des Autoroutes du Nord et de l'Est de la France (SANEF) is running a trial, using a smart card as a subscriber's card, on a section of the toll between Roissy and Survilliers.

In Paris a smart card is being used as a 'smart ticket' on the public transport system. The card can be used either as a season ticket or as a means of paying for individual journeys.

In the UK, Thomas Cook is looking at the use of super smart cards as a frequent-traveller's card. Initially the company will issue a number of these cards to employees for use when they travel. If these trials prove successful the scheme will be extended to business travellers, to give details of itineraries, flight reservations and relevant medical and visa information.

The cardholder will also be able to enter details of expenses in hotels, restaurants, taxis and so on, as they are incurred, and the accumulated details can then be transferred automatically to a company computer on the cardholder's return to the office. It is also possible to store in the card details of entitlement to class of travel, car hire and other facilities determined by the traveller's company, as well as personal preferences such as smoking/non-smoking accommodation.

CASE STUDY

BARCLAYS BANK PROJECT AT DALLINGTON COUNTRY CLUB

In Britain, Barclays Bank's Central Retail Services Division (CRSD), in association with Bull HN, is experimenting with a multi-function smart card for use in the leisure industry. Through its project, at Dallington Country Club, Barclays Bank aims to gain experience with smart card technology and prove EEPROM technology in the public domain. The Bank will be looking at the ways in which the system meets the needs of the leisure administrator and consumer as well as assessing consumer acceptability of the technology. The new card is being phased in gradually, to allow club members time to adjust to the changes. Initially, members were issued with a CP8 card with limited functionality and memory capacity. In August 1989 a replacement card, the CP8 24k EEPROM, was introduced and this has a higher memory capacity and more functions. Services will be added to the card when it is in circulation by activating unused memory areas of the chip.

The 'electronic leisure management system', as depicted in Fig. 10.2, is controlled by a central processor which serves a network of devices including input units, enquiry terminals and off-line point-of-sale terminals. The project, which started in January 1989, is intended to run for 15 months.

The Dallington Country Club is in Northampton and close to the headquarters of Barclays' CRSD. The club is a multi-sport and fitness complex which offers a range of leisure and retail facilities including:

- Squash.
- Fitness area and dance studio.
- Sauna, jacuzzi and steam baths.
- Solarium.
- Bars.
- Restaurant.
- Shop.

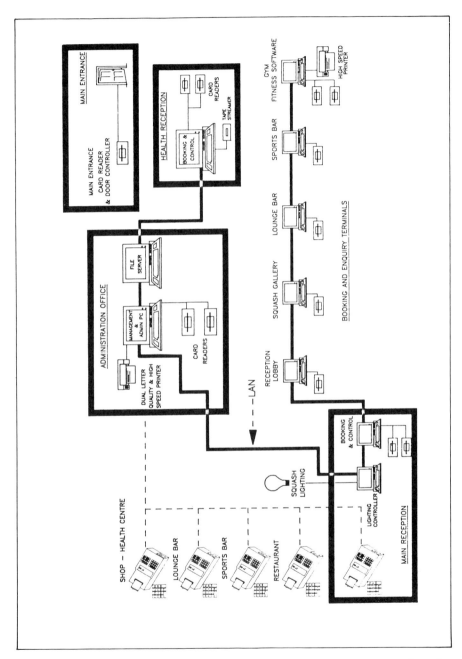

Fig. 10.2. Barclays' electronic leisure management system used at the Dallington Country Club. (Diagram courtesy of Barclays CRSD)

Membership of the club is approximately 2,000 and ages of members range from 6 to 60 years.

The smart card is known as the Dallington Country Club Card. It replaces the club's existing card and incorporates the following eleven functions:

- The card will act as a key, allowing secure access control to the premises when there is no one at reception, perhaps out of hours or at weekends. The cardholder also has to use a PIN to gain entry.
- There are a number of personal computers on the premises, linked together in a local area network. The card allows access to the computer network.
- The customer can change the PIN at a terminal.
- The card holds a static data file of membership details including the cardholder's name, membership number and type of membership.
- Cardholders can choose to store emergency medical data on the card, including details of the member's doctor and personal information such as blood group, normal blood pressure, date of birth, allergies/medical conditions and emergency contact.
- Squash courts can be booked using the card, as in Fig. 10.3. 50% of the cost is debited from the card when the booking is made. The other 50% is debited from the partner when both players come to use the court. The court lights are automatically switched on by a lighting controller terminal connected to the booking and control computer when the play is due to begin. This is conditional upon both players having checked into the club on the day.
- The club has an incentive programme of one free squash game for every six games per month. The card keeps a complete record of transactions so that the free game can be automatically credited to the member's account.
- The card has an electronic purse function which allows funds to be loaded on to the card through cash, cheque or credit card payments at the reception desk. Members can use their cards to pay for goods and services throughout the club, at point-of-sale terminals, as well as to pay for squash courts. The cardholder's PIN is not required for electronic purse transactions but the maximum value for an electronic purse transaction is £5.
- For higher value transactions the card can be used as an electronic cheque. This is mainly used in the restaurant and club shop and the use of a PIN is required.
- The EPROM cards used during the first stages of the project hold a record of all transactions that have been carried out because EPROM

Fig. 10.3. Smart cards can be used at the Dallington Country Club to book squash courts. (Photograph courtesy of Barclays CRSD)

memory cannot be erased. The replacement cards, with advanced EEPROM, hold records of the last 50 transactions.

● Later in the project members will have the option of being able to access information from periodic fitness tests. The card will contain information about the results of the last three fitness assessment tests so that members can review their progress.

For the financial transactions there is a full audit trail. This means that if the card is lost the cash values that are claimed to have been on the card can be verified and transferred to a replacement card.

The benefits of this project to the Dallington Country Club are reduced cash handling, a more efficient booking system and control-led access to premises. To the member, the benefits include a more convenient way of paying for services and booking courts. There are also new services to members, such as the transaction log held on the card, the fitness record, the emergency medical data file and the club's incentive programme.

Barclays Bank says that a further trial, in a completely different field, is now being planned.

11 TELECOMMUNICATIONS APPLICATIONS

SOME TIME ago it was estimated that there were 6.3 million payphones throughout the world and, since then, the number has grown and is continuing to grow. In recent years there has been a move towards replacing coin-operated phones with phones operated by non-intelligent debit cards.

These cards can be purchased in shops and have a range of calling units encoded on them. The caller inserts the card into a slot in the telephone housing and units are deducted from the card according to the length of the call. When all the units are used the card is disposed of. These cards have proved to be popular with the public, because they are convenient, and with the telephone company which no longer has to collect money from the box. Vandalism is reduced as there is no cash to steal.

The smart card now offers a further dimension. It can incorporate a number of telephone call facilities on one card and is more secure than existing telephone cards. Some examples of the facilities that can be incorporated on a smart card, either singly or as a range of options on one card, are described below and on the following pages.

SOME PRINCIPAL USES

PRE-PAID TELEPHONE CARD

The smart card could be purchased with a number of pre-stored calling units, in the same way as existing telephone payment cards. Units would be deducted to pay for calls until the pre-charged value was used up. However, unlike present cards, an EEPROM-based smart card could be recharged.

CREDIT CARD TELEPHONE CARD

As a credit telephone card the smart card could be issued to enable authorised people to make expensive calls. This could be especially useful to business people who travel widely and make extensive use of public telephones. Each card could have its own PIN for use in identifying the cardholder before the call was connected. The value of each call could be logged on the card until a pre-defined credit limit was reached. At that point, the card could, through the telephone system, either inform the telecommunications authority of the amount to be invoiced or authorise a transfer of money from the cardholder's bank account to the authority's account.

SPEED DIALLING

The cardholder could easily store frequently used telephone numbers in the card where short, memorable codes would be allocated to them. When placed in a telephone incorporating a read/write unit a line connection would be made by, simply, keying in the appropriate code.

TELEPHONE PERSONALISATION

The smart card could also be used to personalise telephones to the cardholder's own number. By simply placing a card on a suitably modified telephone incoming calls on the cardholder's phone could be transferred to that number or outgoing calls could be charged to the holder's number. This could be particularly useful when used with a cellular phone installed in a taxi.

CALL LOGGER

People working at home, or away from their usual place of work, could use the smart card to log details of their telephone calls. These details could include number called, duration of call and cost, for use in subsequent expense claims. The card could be interrogated at regular intervals either for claim details or to check that it was only being used for legitimate business purposes.

AUTOMATIC LOG-ON TO INFORMATION SERVICE

The smart card offers a more secure means of granting access to telephone-based information services such as the UK Prestel service.

ACCESS TO TELEPHONE EXCHANGES

The smart card could be issued to telephone maintenance engineers to enable them to gain access to an exchange or to act as a portable data pad for storing details of work undertaken and faults located.

SOME INTERNATIONAL EXAMPLES

Deutsche Bundespost (DBP) began issuing smart cards for use with public cardphones in 1984. The number of cardphones in use is expanding and it is expected that, by the mid-1990s, half the public telephones in GERMANY will be operated by smart cards. Deutsche Bundespost also ran a trial to evaluate the possible use of smart cards to control access to the German videotext system, Bildschirmtext (Btx). The trial was highly successful and, as a result, an experiment in home banking, using smart cards and the Btx system, took place in 1989.

In SWEDEN, in 1989, Televerket, the telecommunications authority, concluded an agreement with Schlumberger for installation of a smart card payphone system. An evaluation by Televerket, comparing other card technologies, showed that smart cards offered the best solution to their needs. The smart card also provides Televerket with interesting possibilities for future applications and services. The agreement covers both the payphones and pre-paid smart cards. In the four-year delivery schedule, 5,000 public payphones and five million cards are to be delivered.

Visa has been testing its super smart card in JAPAN and has placed particular emphasis on developing card services in the field of telephone shopping. The trial is known as VISTA 88 – with VISTA standing for Visa Integrated Services with Telemarketing. The trial began in June 1988. VISTA 88 cardholders used their self-authorising cards to pay for goods in large department stores or to purchase goods from home using especially fitted smart card telephones. Another trial, known as VISTA 89, was planned to include several home banking facilities. This part of the trial will include the Osaka region as well as Tokyo.

In FRANCE paper telephone directories have been replaced by a national videotext system, known as Minitel. The system was introduced to eliminate the cost of producing, updating and distributing the paper directories. The Minitel terminals were distributed free of charge to every home and sold, leased or rented to businesses. It is now possible to have a terminal with a smart card reader attached and some of the services available on Minitel, such as home shopping, are beginning to accept smart cards as a means by which payment is made.

In the UNITED STATES AT&T has tested its contactless 'E' smart card for use with public telephones. AT&T distributed 1,000 cards to frequent business travellers and modified its Public Phone Plus units at 30 airports so that they could be operated by the 'E' card, (see Fig. 11.1). In addition to making telephone calls, cardholders could use the 'E' card to access databases including flight schedules of two airline companies and stock quotation data. Cardholders could also access electronic mail services by using the card.

CASE STUDY

PUBLIC CARDPHONES IN FRANCE

The French telephone network has 25 million lines serving 94% of households throughout the country. There are also 3.8 million videotext terminals (Minitels) in use. By the end of 1987 the total turnover for telecommunications in France had reached 100 billion francs of which 3.8 billion francs was from public telephones.

Fig. 11.1. AT&T contactless smart card telephone. (Photograph courtesy of AT&T)

There are 200,000 public telephones in France. A large number of these, 27,000, are leased from and maintained by French Telecom. The remainder are directly managed by French Telecom, 110,000 of them being by the roadside.

French Telecom has started a programme of replacing existing public telephones with new machines, operated by smart cards, as shown in Fig. 11.2. The French acronym for these is PCAM, which stands for publiphone à carte à memoire. The number of cardphones has increased from 8,000 in 1985 to 45,000 in 1988 and the number is expected to rise to 100,000 by 1990. There are two types of terminals for cardphones – one type is manufactured by Bull and Crouzet as well as Landis and Gyr, while the other type is manufactured by Schlumberger. The policy of French Telecom has been to replace coin-operated telephones with cardphones in places where the use of public telephones was heaviest. This included such places as town

Fig 11.2. French public card telephone. (Photograph courtesy of Schlumberger)

centres, railway stations, harbours, airports and holiday resorts. The telephones can be operated by any one of three different types of cards – a disposable, pre-paid card; a customer card; or a payment card issued by a bank – (see Fig. 11.3)

The pre-paid cards, known as Telecartes, are designed for customers whose needs are less important. The Telecartes can be bought in post offices, tobacco stores or other convenient locations and they are pre-paid in either 40 or 120 telephone units. When all the pre-paid units are used the card is thrown away. These have proved to be popular with the public and sales rose from two million in 1985 to 17 million in 1987 – one journalist has even pointed out that the disposable telephone card has become something of a litter problem in Paris.

The customer card is aimed at users whose communication needs are very important when they are travelling, for instance on business.

The third option is for people who favour a multi-purpose bank

Fig. 11.3. Some pre-paid telephone smart cards in use in France. (Photograph courtesy of Schlumberger)

card. The bank card is issued with 140 pre-paid telephone units. When the number of units drops to 20 the cardholder can purchase more units by pressing a button on the phone and the cost of the units is charged to his bank account. This process can be repeated indefinitely as long as the card lasts and provided that the cardholder's bank account is in good order.

The architecture of the system is based on two levels. The first one permits connection of the cardphones. Its main function is to ensure that maintenance is kept up to date and to collect billing elements. The second level is intended for account consolidation at national level and ensures the interface with billing centres and the information system.

The results of French Telecom's programme of installing cardphones has, so far, been encouraging. Cardphones generated 12.5% of the revenue from public telephones in 1986. This increased to 25% in 1987 and it is expected that, by 1990, the figure will have risen to 50%.

The public has received the cards very well and reception by younger users is particularly good – 78% of users are aged below 35 years. An important benefit of the new cards, to both Telecom and the public alike, is the reduction in the amount of vandalism. The monthly rate of payphones out of order has decreased from 12% in 1984, before cardphones were introduced, to 3% in 1987.

The cardphones have been promoted in a campaign which has included advertising posters and television spots. French Telecom also sells advertising space on cardphones – advertisements can either be for products or as promotions for artists.

The first stage of the cardphone programme has given priority to the installation of cardphones on the public highway. However, in a second stage, cardphones, leased from and maintained by French Telecom, will be marketed for use in private premises.

12 OTHER APPLICATIONS

IN THE major areas of smart card applications, which were discussed in the previous chapters, there has been a great deal of activity and some projects have gone beyond the trial stage into full implementation. There are, however, many other areas where smart cards could be useful and, in some less obvious applications, they are already in use.

SOME PRINCIPAL USES

MILITARY APPLICATIONS

In the area of military applications, where strong security is vital, the smart card can perform a variety of functions. Some of these are outlined in the following paragraphs.

Personnel access control

The most common devices used to control access of personnel, to areas where sensitive work is carried out or where data is held, are keys, badges and magnetic cards. These all have the same basic disadvantages: they can easily be duplicated; and, when stolen or passed on, they can allow entry by an unauthorised person. The smart card overcomes these weaknesses by being difficult to reproduce and capable of storing a digitised personal characteristic as described in Chapter 7. With suitable verification equipment, this data can be used at the point of entry to identify whether the user is the authorised cardholder. The card can also be individually personalised to allow access to limited facilities, depending on the holder's security clearance. A log of the holder's movements, through a security system, can be stored on the card as a security audit trail.

Portable data file

The largest application for the smart card in the military sector is likely to be the personal data file. All military personnel could carry a card containing personal details, medical records, financial records and details of privileges, such as access to officers' recreational facilities. The card could also be programmed to allow the holder access to various parts of a military site, depending upon rank.

Military personnel are constantly moving from one base to another and, if the smart card travelled with each individual, this would allow personal records to be viewed instantly upon arrival at a new base – saving administrative costs. Contactless smart cards could be particularly useful in this context as they could be produced in the dog-tag format shown in Fig. 12.1, already familiar to military personnel.

Equipment record

High-value weapons, such as torpedoes, have a storage life of a number of years and have documentation associated with them which must be regularly updated to include such items as servicing information. The smart card could be physically attached to the weapon to act as a log-book, offering savings in documentation and, more importantly, provide greater logistic control through its in-built ability to be linked to a computer through a read/write unit.

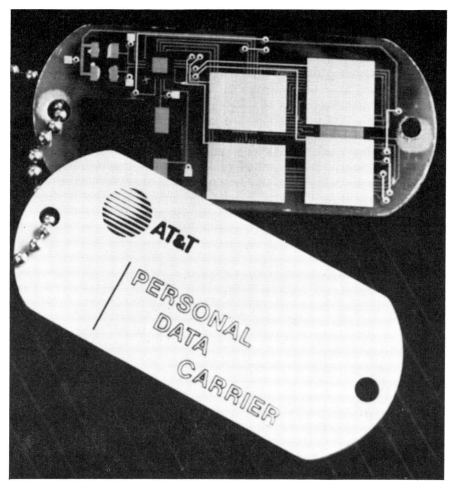

Fig. 12.1. The AT&T contactless smart card repackaged in a rigid dog-tag format suitable for use as a personal military data file. (Photograph courtesy of AT&T)

Other military applications

Other military applications for the smart card include control of photocopying machines in secure areas – to prevent unauthorised copying of confidential documents, storage of frequency-hopping radio data and the recording of fuel issued for military vehicles.

INDUSTRIAL APPLICATIONS

Manufacturing industry

In an industrial setting the smart card can have many applications. It can be used to program computerised numerically-controlled machines, replacing punched cards or magnetic tape.

On a production line the card can be attached to a product being manufactured and used to store a record of the progress of the item throughout the stages of its manufacture (see Fig. 12.2).

In the car manufacturing industry, for instance, a smart card can be attached to each vehicle and used to store records of work to be carried out. It can accompany the vehicle through the complete manufacturing process. The card can then remain with the car when it is sold and act as a smart log, containing a complete history of the car, including maintenance data.

Fig. 12.2. On a production line the smart card can be used to store a record of the progress of manufactured goods. (Photograph courtesy of GEC)

Computer industry

There are several important smart card application areas in the computer industry. For instance, one of the problems facing software producers is the ease with which software can be copied. Illegal copying is most common at the lower end of the market where programs, particularly games programs, for personal microcomputers are passed from one user to another and several copies are probably made from one original. Despite the size of the problem, no agreement has been reached between computer manufacturers and software producers on measures to combat software piracy.

The smart card could be used to prevent illegal copying. Part of the software to be sold could be stored on the card so that the program would not run without the card being present. Any illegal copies of the program would, therefore, be useless. The high-security features of the smart card would make it impossible for anyone to discover exactly what was on the card and duplicate it.

The introduction of these security measures is likely to be influenced by the costs of the smart cards and read/write units but is a promising way of protecting software.

The use of the smart card in controlling personal access to dangerous or sensitive areas has been discussed before in connection with medical and military applications. However, an important application of the smart card is in controlling access to sensitive information held on computers. The card can be programmed to enable the holder to enter various areas of a database, depending on his level of authority. It may, for instance, allow someone to view information but not alter it. Access to computer networks can also be made highly secure using smart cards.

AUTOMOTIVE APPLICATIONS

One worry, faced by all car owners, is the ever increasing number of car thefts. The use of a smart card key can improve car security by having a unique personal code stored in it, which would be needed to open the doors of the vehicle and start the engine. While not able to prevent all break-ins, this would make the car very much more difficult to steal. The card could work with on-board systems to automatically change the position of the seat and mirrors to suit the individual driver and tune the radio to the cardholder's favourite channel. Vital information about the driver, such as blood group and other important medical details, could also be stored in the card at the same time for emergency use.

In-car systems, such as cellular radio telephones and route guidance systems, are usually rented. Rental payments could be made by the use of a smart card and the card could also control access to the system.

Roadside parking meters are a source of expense and inconvenience to local authorities and of frustration to motorists. Smart cards can help here with in-car meters which deduct parking charge units from the card when inserted in the meter, while the vehicle is parked. This system is coming into use in several European countries and Fig. 12.3. shows an example of one such meter which is discussed fully in a later section.

Fig. 12.3. Piaf personal parking meter in use at Saint-Brieuc, France. (Photograph courtesy of Groupe Innovatron)

There are other potential automotive applications of smart cards. Businesses using company cars may find that fleet management can be made more efficient by using a smart card to record information pertaining to an individual car. This smart log would be kept with the car and could contain, for example, information concerning maintenance, road tax, insurance, users and fuel consumption. This would make record keeping for fleet cars much simpler and more reliable.

In the road haulage industry the smart card could be used to control access to loading depots and carry information on loads and destinations. It could also be used to monitor the fuel consumption of a lorry.

AIRPORT SECURITY APPLICATIONS

An important issue in all airports today is security. The smart card can provide secure access control to buildings or computer terminals and it is particularly suitable in large or scattered locations as there is no need for expensive cabling between a central processor and the various entry terminals on doors and barriers. Personnel would be issued with cards programmed only to allow them access to buildings and terminals necessary for their work. The card itself can log movements of personnel in secure or restricted areas. This would, typically, include not only details of the date, time and frequency of successful admissions to those areas, but also the dates and times of unsuccessful attempts to gain entry, together with the identity numbers of the cards involved.

POSTAL APPLICATIONS

There are a number of postal applications for smart cards. They could store (in an electronic form) licences that are normally purchased at a post office, or be used for postal savings accounts and for stamp purchasing. Letter and parcel franking machines which operate using smart cards have already been developed (see Fig. 12.4). The card is charged with a monetary value and the franking machine will only operate when the card is inserted. A value is deducted from the card each time a letter is franked. When EEPROM-based smart cards are used in this application they can be recharged when empty. For extra security the card could be programmed to work only with a particular machine.

Fig. 12.4. The Pitney Bowes Smart Postage Dispenser – a smart card operated letter franking machine. (Photograph courtesy of Pitney Bowes)

THE 'TOWN CARD'

The idea of using a single smart card as a 'town card', giving access to a variety of services such as sports facilities, theatres and buses run by the local authority, is coming into being. The card could give benefits to local residents such as preferential access to sports facilities and give the residents a greater feeling of belonging to a town.

EDUCATION AND EMPLOYMENT

Smart cards are beginning to be used by universities and colleges to store details of registration, attendance and academic progress, and to give access to information about career opportunities. There are a variety of applications in this area where smart cards could be used.

SOME INTERNATIONAL EXAMPLES

The UNITED STATES Department of Defense began issuing smart identity/eligibility cards, on a small scale, to military personnel in 1984. The cards controlled access to medical, recreational and other benefits which had previously been open to waste and fraud. It has been reported that the department has been impressed with the smart card's security features and may well issue the cards on a much larger scale, to military personnel, in the future.

Smart cards are being used by Nissei Plastic Kogyo in JAPAN to instruct numerically-controlled milling machines. The smart cards hold information on plastic injection moulding – one card can hold information for 10 moulds. Hitachi Seiki Company has also developed a smart card system, for transferring and storing numerical control programmes for machine tools, and Kyodo is using a smart card in personnel management and inventory control.

In 1988, camera manufacturer Minolta introduced a camera which uses smart cards to supply it with different photographic functions to provide automatic settings for various conditions of lighting and so on. The card fits into a slot at the side of the camera.

An ingenious alternative to the roadside parking meter has been introduced by the local authorities of Saint-Brieuc and Metz in FRANCE. Known as the Piaf and marketed by the Innovatron Group, it is a personal parking meter the size of a pocket calculator, which is placed on the dashboard of a car (see Fig. 12.3). It is used in conjunction with a pre-paid smart card. The driver simply inserts the card into a slot in the Piaf and presses a button on the meter to select the appropriate parking zone. The zone number flashes on the screen alternating with the time, the device's identification number and a code (based on the day's date) produced by a secret algorithm. These displays allow the driver and the traffic warden to verify that the Piaf is working correctly. The driver places the Piaf on the dashboard so that the screen is visible from outside.

The Piaf calculates the number of parking units to be debited according to the particular municipality's parking regulations. It can take account of the time of day, the day of the week, length of stay permitted and so on. For example, if a driver parks a car late in the morning in a zone where parking is free between 12:00 and 14:00, the Piaf will turn off automatically at noon. On returning to the car the driver simply removes the smart card which can be used repeatedly until all the units have been consumed.

At Saint-Brieuc, Piaf has resolved a large number of problems encountered by municipal management in the domain of parking regulations. In particular, the collection of parking fees is greatly simplified by the pre-payment formula, and the risk of theft or fraud is practically eliminated. The card and the Piaf carry the city's coat of arms, enhancing its image, and the card can also be printed with general information. The space can even be rented to advertisers as the card is kept until all its units are used.

The card is used in a similar way to the French telephone cards. It can be bought containing 50, 100 or 200 units and is discarded when all the units have been used up. If the card reaches the end of its credit while in use, the Piaf stops and displays the time at which it stopped. The same happens when the maximum authorised parking time has been reached.

User reactions to the Piaf system have been strongly favourable. A survey carried out at Saint-Brieuc revealed that 87% of users were totally satisfied with the system and less than 1% expressed little or no satisfaction. Asked what qualities pleased them about Piaf, 59% said that they no longer needed to have change for the parking meter, 35% said that it freed them from worry, 21% said that it resulted in fewer fines, 21% commended it as practical and 7% said that it saved time.

The system was first used experimentally at Saint-Brieuc, in March 1988, and was put into full use in September of that year. Negotiations are in progress with Stockholm, Gothenburg and Malmö, in Sweden, with the Credit Communal de Belgique, for a national system, and with other authorities both in France and internationally.

A national commercial driver's licence scheme is scheduled to be introduced in the USA during the next few years and the state of Wisconsin has proposed the use of a smart card carrying personal details and details of the vehicle, together with a biometric personal identifier. The front of the card will carry a digitised photograph of the holder, providing the visual identification often required when cashing a cheque in the USA. The first cards of this type are due to be issued in 1990. Extensions of the system could, ultimately, lead to the the card being used as identification in renewing vehicle licence plates and as proof of ownership when selling a vehicle.

In ITALY it is planned to use smart cards as a payment device on toll motorways. AT&T cards can be used in a system which will enable drivers to pass through the tolls without stopping. Drivers are required to slow down to about 20mph, but do not need to stop. An antenna scans a unit into which the smart card is inserted for information from the card which is transmitted to a remote accounting centre for debiting. Work is said to be in progress on a system which would read data from cars travelling as fast as 120mph.

The smart card is used by the SENEGALESE customs to control duties owed by various transport companies. Each card is given the forwarding agent's name and has a monetary value loaded on to it. As the goods pass through customs, the card is debited.

In JAPAN Kyodo Oil, in co-operation with Toshiba and the Mitsui Bank, is also experimenting with smart cards at Kyodo's Tama service centre outside Tokyo. Customers use a smart card to pay for petrol at the station. In addition to storing details of sales, the card also stores details of periodic inspections of the car, functioning like an electronic log book. The data provided through the cards also helps to manage merchandise and customer service.

A large car leasing firm has decided to use a smart card vehicle management system. The cards will hold complete vehicle records which will be updated using read/write units at 100 repair centres and 1,300 maintenance shops. The system will expand to cover fuel and merchandise sales.

Another company, Osaka Toyota, is using smart cards to record purchase conditions, maintenance, inspection and insurance data for new cars in 41 outlets.

In the UK, Folkestone Ferry are using GEC contactless smart cards, in a tag format, to ensure safe loading of ferries. Lorries boarding the cross channel ferry are required to collect a tag at the security gate. Information, such as identity number and lorry registration number, is entered into the tag and the lorry proceeds to an unmanned weighbridge where the tag is read and the data collated with the vehicle's weight.

Smart cards are being linked experimentally with electronic data interchange (EDI), in the USA, to improve the accuracy of deliveries to major supermarket chains. The trial is known as DEX/UCS – direct exchange/uniform communications standard – and its aim is to ensure that all the information about a delivery is transferred by the supplier into a smart card which the driver takes with him.

At the receiving store the card is inserted into a terminal, at the loading bay, and the information is transferred automatically into the recipient's stock record system. The list of items is also displayed or printed so that the delivery can be checked. A separate card can be supplied for each store or, alternatively, all the details for deliveries in a single day can be stored in one card. Seven supermarket chains are participating in the trial, with a number of major suppliers, and the system is expected to be implemented on a large scale in the early 1990s.

Vitrolles in FRANCE is one town which has taken up the concept of a smart card as a town card. Local residents have been given cards which allow them access to various services. The cards used are manufactured by Gemplus.

In ITALY universities are issuing students with smart cards in which they can record information about registration, attendance and merit certificates using self-service terminals. Faculty members have similar cards programmed to record examination results at a large number of special terminals.

The state of Michigan, in the UNITED STATES, has introduced an 'opportunity card', developed by the Applied Systems Institute, using Schlumberger smart cards and terminals. Initially, it is being used in the state's community colleges to give students access to courses that are available to them. The card provides secure areas for sensitive information, accessible only to the bearer using a PIN, and for recording transactions as well as an accessible area for changing information.

The card carries relevant data on the individual and can interact, via a reader, with a computer at the community college office which holds information on courses and so on. The cardholder can find out what courses are available, given the eligibility data stored in the card. The system will indicate where the student should go and provide budgeting limits which may be involved. The card can also include the individual's employment plans and information on current skills, past experience, aptitudes and scores from standard tests.

It is intended that the card will be made available in the near future to all Michigan residents who want to learn about new career opportunities and improve their skills throughout their working years.

CASE STUDY

PEANUT BUYING POINT AUTOMATION PROJECT, USA

One of the biggest smart card applications, to date, has been in the agricultural industry in the USA. The vast American peanut harvest, which takes place mainly in the southern states, has been computerised over the past few years using smart cards.

Peanut farming in the USA is controlled by price-support legislation and, under this legislation, the US Department of Agriculture (USDA) can control the amount of peanuts grown. In return, the farmers are paid a guaranteed price for every pound of peanuts harvested under a peanut farm's poundage quota.

The price-support programme is complex and, until 1987, the Agricultural Stabilization and Conservation Service (ASCS) had to monitor the programme by relying on paper files kept, for each peanut farm, at ASCS county offices throughout the south and south west. However, with 56,000 peanut producers, more than 500 buying points and 400,000 six-part forms to process each year, it was becoming increasingly difficult to deal efficiently with the paperwork. The USDA decided to find a way of automating the system so that administrative costs could be reduced and efficiency improved.

In 1985, a one-month feasibility study of a system of automated peanut buying points was conducted by the Applied Systems Institute (ASI). A successful test, at five locations, led to a wider pilot test in 1986. Smart cards were used to maintain the farmers' marketing records and contained information such as: the farmer's name; farm number; peanut quota in pounds; crop loan eligibility information; and transaction records. The automated system was tested in six states by 46 buying points and, as a result of the success of these tests, the USDA, together with ASI, automated all buying points in 1987.

Fig. 12.5. A peanut buying point in Pleasanton, Texas. (Photograph courtesy of Agricultural Stabilization and Conservation Service)

The equipment for the 1987 implementation was provided, primarily, by the ASCS. Buying points without existing automation equipment were provided with: an IBM PC/XT personal computer; software, written by ASI and IBM, to automate the marketing process and transmit the results to ASCS state computers; and a read/write unit to read and update the marketing smart card brought in by the producer, Fig. 12.5. Micro Card Technologies, Inc. (MCTI), provided the smart cards, which had enough memory for about 50 market transactions. This allowed nearly all producers to complete the season using one card.

Buying points which already had automation equipment were allowed to keep their existing systems and ASI modified the software to work on them. A smart card read/write unit was provided for each of these systems.

Co-ordinating the delivery and installation of the systems for a project of this size required careful planning. The IBM warehouse in Mechanicsburg, Pennsylvania, became the staging site for hardware deliveries – mainly to buying points but also to some county offices and training sites. The equipment was sent by three different vendors to Mechanicsburg where IBM staff were responsible for testing hardware, uploading application software received from ASI, repackaging consolidated units and shipping the units to a designated end-user by a specific date. A total of 460 units were shipped from Mechanicsburg and there were problems with 60 shipments – over half of these were late deliveries.

On the whole, the co-ordination of the deliveries by IBM staff was considered to be successful but two main areas of weakness were identified: control and accountability of on-site operations; and flexibility and responsiveness. In future there will be: a written quality control procedure, supervised by an on-site representative of the prime contractor; direct communications between the prime contractor and the staging site manager; and more rigorous testing of all equipment options prior to shipment.

From the point of view of shipping logistics, it was found that not enough lead-time had been allowed, before the beginning of live operations, to correct any problems that might occur with either the delivery or equipment. A minimum of 30 days was considered necessary for this. It has been suggested that the problems encountered with deliveries to rural areas might have been alleviated by giving shipping companies addresses which were as precise as possible. Some buying points were very remote and difficult to find. It was decided that, in future, training equipment deliveries would be simplified by having fewer training centres. More training and written instructions would be given to those repacking the equipment for shipping.

The distribution of smart cards was less problematic than the shipments of hardware. The major problem occurred before distribution. The card manufacturer, MCTI, had agreed to send the cards in serial number order with a print-out of the numbers in each box of cards. A pre-shipment test, by ASI, found that the cards were not in order and did not necessarily match the numbers on the print-out. As a result, the serial numbers for 60,000 cards had to be read and printed out. MCTI provided ASI with the software to do this, using a personal computer, and ASI provided the staff.

There was also a problem with the packaging of the cards for shipment. The cards were kept in serial number order by rubber bands and mailed inside padded envelopes. However, in several shipments the rubber bands broke and the cards arrived at their destination out of order. The serial numbers were encoded in the cards and were not visible on the outside of the card, so returning the cards to serial number order was a potentially time-consuming task for the county office, depending on the number of cards involved. In future, special-size boxes will be used to ship the smart cards.

Application software for the buying points.

The software used in the 1987 implementation was based on that used in the 1986 pilot test prototype, but incorporating improvements suggested by the government, industry and ASI technical staff. The main functions of the system for the buying points included: data entry; form processing; display and update of the marketing smart card; and daily data transmission. The 1987 system had increased processing speed and enhanced editing capabilities over the 1986 prototype system. Several new features were added which increased the complexity of the software and its potential for creating problems. As a result of this, the software went through six releases during the 1987 marketing season.

Once it had been accepted that the software met the operational requirements of the government, a field test was run in three selected buying points: Jackson, North Carolina; Portales, New Mexico; and Enterprise, Alabama. The aim of the field test was to demonstrate that the buying point system could operate in realistic situations and carry out normal processing routines as well as some more unusual marketing transactions.

One experienced buying point operator from each region was brought in to test the systems. The Applied Systems Institute hoped that this would expose any errors or difficulties with the software that had not been noticed in previous tests. While the software was being evaluated in these field tests, IBM's usability laboratory took the opportunity to study the user-friendliness of the system as a whole.

In June 1987 a final test was run to check that peanut marketing data could be accurately sent from the buying points to the county offices via electronic transmission. The transmitted data were found to be correct with only one or two problem areas which were corrected.

Application software for the county offices.

The introduction of the marketing smart card meant that special software was required. COBOL programs were developed by ASI for the IBM System 36 which was to be used in county offices. These programs enabled the county operator to: personalise the marketing smart cards; correct, update and recreate marketing smart cards; and reconcile marketing smart card records with the paper forms for each producer. After acceptance testing, which included creating, updating and personalising a marketing smart card, the software was field tested, in six counties in five states. The software for the county office system 36 was able to draw data from eight master files containing information such as: the farm producer file; the contract file; the producer name and address file; and peanut quota transfer file.

The performance of the software during the season was considered successful by most users. There were few serious problems with the software at buying points and these were quickly corrected. The industry was generally in favour of improving the software for the 1988 season.

Hardware

The hardware selected for the 1987 project was based on the hardware used in the pilot test in 1986. This included the IBM PC/XT with 640k memory, an IBM 2400 baud modem for transmitting data down the telephone line, a Fujitsu printer, an input/output (I/O) box, security cards and marketing smart cards.

A survey of buying point operators revealed that although many hardware problems occurred, 85% of these were corrected in a quick or timely fashion. Many operators had found that replacement units were available and that the replacement procedure worked satisfactorily.

Card I/O device failures

During the 1987 season approximately 10% of the card reading devices were returned to MCTI with problems. MCTI analysed the problems as shown in Fig. 12.6.

The I/O devices were found to be vulnerable to changes in the power supply, particularly to power failures which are not uncommon in the buying point environment. A power failure resulted in a loss of firmware – a combination of hardware and software – which temporarily deactivated the device. Operators were able to restore the firmware themselves so it is not known how many times this problem occurred.

Problem	No. of readers	Percentage of readers
Reset BRAMS*	36	38%
Hardware defect	24	26%
Power supply	14	15%
Card connector	12	13%
Unknown or mistake	6	6%
Interface cable	2	2%
TOTAL	94	100%

* Battery Random Access Memory

Fig. 12.6 Analysis of problems with card readers

Smart card failures

The 1987 project used approximately 74,000 smart cards and, of these, only 109 (less than 1%) were returned to MCTI after pre-distribution testing found them to be defective. However, after distribution, more cards were found to be defective or were subsequently damaged. A total of 649 cards were returned to ASI as inoperable but only 149 of these were found to be defective. Of the remainder, some were classed as 'empty', because they had never been personalised, some contained garbage data, resulting from a problem with the personalisation process, and 205 were found to be functioning normally. The analysis showed an extremely low error rate, confirming the reliability of the smart cards.

Printer failures

The Fujitsu printer, purchased for the 1987 project, was designed with a push-feed system. This was found to be susceptible to jamming when the six-part peanut marketing forms were fed through. The forms were, apparently, too thick and loosely constructed to feed smoothly through the printer. ASI received a number of complaints about jamming and, in some places, 50% of forms were wasted as a result.

Other problems experienced with the printer were largely due to operator error. Two common mistakes were: setting the switches incorrectly; and selecting the wrong printer configuration.

Training

The 1987 project paid great attention to training staff to make full and efficient use of the buying point automation system. The two groups specifically targeted for government-provided training were the buying point operators, using the government system, and county and state ASCS personnel, providing first-line technical support.

The training objectives included the following:

- To understand the role and responsibilities of the buying point operator.
- To install and de-install the system.
- To prepare the system for processing peanut sales transactions, using ASI's pre-processing modules.
- To perform daily processing functions, such as: key entry of grading and sales data; saving data from marketing forms in a hard disk file; and updating the producer marketing smart card.
- To perform telecommunications functions to enable peanut data to be transmitted to state ASCS offices.
- To handle problems, such as data recovery following a hard disk crash, to carry out basic hardware diagnosis and to recover from power-failures.
- To instil operator confidence and self-reliance.

Training sessions were organised in three regions from May to August. Professional trainers were recruited – to write the curricula and conduct the sessions for buying point and county personnel – to ensure that the training was of a high quality.

The training programme included 47 workshops which were attended by 962 trainees. The workshops were conducted by eight professional trainers who had been given two weeks of formal training on the peanut automation system. They were provided with training materials, developed specifically for the programme, in the form of audio-visual aids and hand-outs as well as having the use of ASI facilities for individual practice.

The training curricula provided a great deal of 'hands-on' experience, particularly in unpacking equipment, installing hardware and software, operating the system and repacking the equipment. A complete automated system was provided by ASI for every two trainees. A maximum of two representatives from each buying point was allowed on the training programme.

In 1988 it was anticipated that training would be aimed mainly at buying point operators and that county office personnel would not receive any further formal training. The training objectives for 1988 included:

- To widen training to include operators.
- To put greater emphasis on telecommunications, card handling, backing-up procedures and basic trouble-shooting.
- To encourage the Growers Association to participate actively in training and increase its members' knowledge of the buying point system.
- To prepare more realistic training exercises.

The training carried out in 1987 was designed specifically for the first year of implementation for the whole industry. With the system established, training then focused on first-year operators, with a refresher course for experienced operators.

Documentation

The manuals for the buying point and county office systems were prepared by ASI. Interim buying point manuals were prepared in April and May 1987, for use in training. The first version of the completed manual was distributed in August but a new version was produced in October, following software revisions. The county offices received personalisation reference manuals which explained the functions and procedures for using the county personalisation software. However, the buying point manual was the more important, from the point of view of supporting the implementation of the project.

A survey, conducted by ASI, showed that the majority of operators made great use of the manual as a learning tool. They had, however, found some sections of the book confusing, particularly the section on telecommunications. Operators were questioned about possible additions to the manual and, unanimously, agreed that there should be a section dealing with 'possible problems'. During the 1987 season 94% of operators said that, when a problem occurred, they referred to the manual first before calling for help.

During the 1987 season ASI provided a technical assistance centre to offer support to the buying point operators. A log was kept of calls received by the centre and of the way in which the problem was resolved. Analysis of these calls showed that 30% of problems were caused by operator errors which, it was believed, could be reduced by improving those sections of the manual dealing with the most common problem areas. This would also make it easier for operators to correct mistakes by themselves.

Telecommunications

The USDA has a mandatory data communications contract with GTE Telenet, called DEPNET, and the government required that the peanut buying automation system should enable each buying point to communicate data to state and county offices using DEPNET. The contract for the development of software to interface DEPNET with the buying point application software was awarded to IBM and a prototype was tested in the 1986 pilot test.

In the 1987 implementation, peanut transaction data was stored in the buying point computers during the day. Access to the State and County Office Automation Project (SCOAP), computer was through a security smart card. The call to the Telenet network was initiated by either the buying point operator or the application software. The caller signed on to the network, with security codes contained in the smart card, and issued a connect address to the state office's IBM System 36 computer. When the connection had been made, additional user identifications and passwords were exchanged and, when validated as a legitimate user, control passed to software which performed file transfers between the buying point computer and the state's System 36. All sales data went to the state computer which then distributed the sales records to the producers' relevant home county System 36.

If telecommunications failed, the back-up procedure for the buying points was to send a back-up diskette to the local county office for shipment consolidation to the state office. Each state office had an IBM PC/XT computer attached to the state computer to input back-up diskettes. The standard software enabling the PC/XT to transfer data from diskette to the state computer was found to be too slow and complicated so ASI developed special software to streamline and speed up the procedures.

There were telecommunications failures during the 1987 season, some of them, particularly in the south west, due to poor telephone lines. The impact of telecommunications failures would have been minimised if the back-up system had worked properly. However, the back-up diskettes were often unusable. Some of the reasons for this were as follows:

● They were unformatted or formatted by incompatible computers.
● They were formatted but blank.
● They had I/O errors and were damaged.

When incorrect diskettes were sent the procedure was for the buying point to send a replacement telecommunications back-up diskette to the state office. Unfortunately, owing to the delay in notifying the buying points of mistakes, the replacement disk had sometimes been re-used and, as a result, these transmission files became missing electronic data which required special recovery by ASI personnel.

In an attempt to reduce the number of invalid back-up diskettes, ASI produced and distributed an information sheet for buying point operators. This distinguished between different types of back-ups, such as telecommunications, data and system, and how to handle each. The buying point operator was also instructed to run a directory of the telecommunications back-up before mailing, to be certain that the files were correct. The problem with invalid diskettes was aggravated by the amount of time that state computers were down. If the state computer was down the buying points were unable to transmit data directly and the potential number of invalid diskettes increased.

GLOSSARY OF TERMS

algorithm   Predefined set of processes or rules for the solution of a problem.

amplitude modulation   Means of transmitting binary data by varying the amplitude of a constant frequency between two levels, one level representing a binary 1, the other representing a binary 0.

application program   Set of instructions stored in the memory of a smart card or microcomputer which is dedicated to a specific user task, such as a financial payment, as opposed to a general purpose or supervisory program.

authenticator   Means by which communicating devices, such as a smart card and read/write unit, verify the identity of each other.

automatic teller machine (ATM)   Machine which allows bank and building society customers to withdraw money from their accounts and carry out other financial functions, such as presenting cheques for payment into an account.

back lapping   Process by which a wafer is ground on its underside to reduce its thickness.

baud   Term commonly used in communications. A baud defines the number of bits transmitted per second; for example, 10 bauds is equivalent to 10 bits per second.

binary   Counting system which uses only the digits 1 and 0.

biometrics   Very secure means of identifying a person, based on a physical characteristic of the person such as a fingerprint. The identification of a person by a signature also comes under the category of biometrics.

bit   Abbreviation of 'binary digit'. A bit can be either 1 or 0.

bumping   Process by which layers are grown on the connection pads of a chip to raise them above the surface of the rest of the chip.

byte   Eight bits grouped together and considered as a single entity.

capacitive coupling   This is a technique which can be used for contactless smart card operation. It is based on the principle that, by applying a voltage to a pair of conductors just below the surface of a smart card, an electrical field is formed which extends beyond the surface of the card. The field can induce a charge on a second pair of conductors in the read/write unit. The presence or absence of a charge on the second pair of conductors represents the transmission of a binary 1 or 0. Using the same principle, data can also be transmitted to the card from the read/write unit.

chip   Electronic circuit, containing as many as 100,000 transistors, which has been fabricated on a piece of silicon, typically less than 1 centimetre square. Also known as an integrated circuit (IC).

complementary metal oxide semiconductor (CMOS)   Chips can be fabricated in various technologies. CMOS is a popular technology for smart card chips, primarily because it requires very little power and has good immunity to electrical noise (interference).

contactless smart card   Smart card which is capable of working with a read/write unit without direct physical connection between the two.

contact smart card   Smart card which receives electrical power and transmits and receives data, via a metallic contact on its surface.

corporate cash management   Term used by banks, for a scheme which allows larger customers to have access to the bank's computer, from a remote computer via the telephone network, to allow the customers to view their accounts and move money between their accounts.

custom ROM   See **masking**.

data encryption standard (DES)   Method of encryption originating from IBM and adopted by the National Bureau of Standards, part of the US Department of Commerce. DES consists of a published algorithm, which defines the procedure for encrypting, and keys, which provide the uniqueness for the encryption. The same key is used for encryption and decryption.

decryption   Method, according to a set of rules, for reconstituting an encrypted message into readable form.

direct broadcasting by satellite (DBS)   The transmission of television pictures to homes, via a satellite. Often used in the context of pay television.

electrically programmable, read-only memory (EPROM)   Memory which retains its contents when the power is removed and which can be both read from and written to. EPROM memory can only be erased by exposing it to ultraviolet light through a quartz lid and, for this reason, it cannot be erased when used in a smart card. Thus, it can only be programmed once and, in some smart card applications, is discarded after all the memory locations are full.

electronically erasable, programmable read-only memory (EEPROM, E^{2}PROM)   Memory which retains its contents when power is removed and which can be both read from and written to. It can be reprogrammed by electrical means.

electronic cash   Also known as electronic purse. A small monetary value stored, electronically, in a smart card which can be used to purchase goods or services, the value of the transaction being deducted from the card.

electronic cheque   Form of electronic funds transfer between accounts (see **electronic fund transfer at the point-of-sale**) in which, the smart card acts as a secure identification token which, in conjunction with the entry of a correct PIN, can authorise the transfer of funds.

electronic fund transfer at the point-of-sale (EFTPOS)   Payment for goods at a retail outlet by the automatic transfer of funds from the purchaser's bank account to the retailer's bank account.

electronic purse   See **electronic cash.**

electronic traveller's cheque   Smart card equivalent of the traveller's cheque. A pre-paid monetary value is stored in the card, possibly in foreign currency. In conjunction with a PIN, purchases can be made using the card by deducting the appropriate value from the card. The reconciliation of the values deducted (traveller's cheques) held in the terminal is carried out at a later time.

emulator   Fault-finding tool used in the development of software. It usually comprises a board or computer which can behave exactly like another computer, such as the microcomputer in a smart card. It is loaded with the software that is to be tested and allows the software to be stopped at various points during its execution. Thus checks can be made on, for example, memory contents to see if the software is functioning as expected.

encryption   Method whereby data to be transmitted is made unintelligible (scrambled) using a set of rules and which can be made intelligible again after transmissions by the recipient to whom the message is intended and not by an unauthorised person.

Fiat Shamir technique   Method of public key encryption, devised by Fiat and Shamir, which is much faster than the more widely known RSA method and requires less program memory. It is based on a technique known as zero knowledge proof.

frequency modulation, frequency shift keying   Means of transmitting data in which the digits 1 and 0 are represented as two different frequencies.

glob topping   The covering of a chip with a material to protect it from chemicals that can be generated within the PVC of a card.

hot card file   List of lost and stolen cards which are no longer valid.

inductive coupling   Process which involves two coils of wire. When an alternating current is passed through one coil an alternating magnetic field is created. When the other coil is brought in close proximity the alternating magnetic field induces a flow of current in it. This technique can be slightly modified to allow data as well as power to be transmitted between the coils. It is a technique which is used for contactless smart card operation.

injection moulding   Manufacturing method for producing small plastic articles by heating granules of plastic until they melt and then injecting the resultant liquid into a mould under pressure at, typically, 300°C. When the plastic cools it sets, having taken up the shape of the mould, which could be in a card shape.

inner lead bonding   Process used in tape automated bonding which connects the chip's bumped bonding pads to tape.

instruction set   The set of instructions that can be executed by the central processing unit of a computer or a microprocessor.

integrated circuit (IC)   See **chip.**

International Standards Organisation (ISO)   The forum at which representatives from different countries meet to agree standards for worldwide use.

interrogator   Device which interrogates a tag by sending out a transmission (usually radio frequency) to which the tag sends back a response. Also known as a scanner.

key   Parameter of an encryption algorithm. The algorithm, when fed with data, results in a scrambled output of that data. The use of the key is such that, if it is obtained by a person intent on fraud, the key can be changed without the need to change the algorithm.

key management   The process of generating, issuing and protecting the keys used in encryption.

lamination   Traditional method for making plastic cards which entails the bonding together of layers of thin PVC sheets, usually three or four, by the application of heat and pressure.

laser card   See **optical memory card.**

magnetic stripe card   The plastic card with a magnetic stripe which is used internationally for financial transactions. The magnetic stripe contains three tracks: one designated for the airline industry, the second for financial transactions; the third, which was a later addition, is the only track that can be rewritten and is intended for use in off-line financial transactions.

masking   The process of embedding software in ROM during the manufacture of the chip by connecting certain circuit elements together to a pattern defined by the software. Also known as customising the ROM when the software to be embedded in the chip is for a specific application, defined by the supplier of the end product in which the ROM is to be incorporated.

memory card   Card similar to a smart card, although usually thicker, which has very little or no processing ability but contains a large amount of memory in the form of a number of chips.

microcomputer   Computer containing a processor and memory on a single chip. Not to be confused with a personal computer which is often referred to as a microcomputer. Also known as a micro-controller.

microcontroller   See **microcomputer.**

micromodule   The chip, together with the substrate (circuit) on which it is mounted, which is embedded in a smart card.

microprocessor   The central processing part of a microcomputer. The microprocessor can either be incorporated as part of a microcomputer chip or be a separate chip. It is able to manipulate and interpret data according to a set of instructions stored in memory (program).

Minitel   Low-cost mass produced terminal (including display) which was introduced in France to eliminate the cost of producing, updating and distributing paper telephone directories. Minitel terminals are distributed free of charge, for home use, and sold, leased or rented to businesses. They are now being used in many more applications.

monochip   If a smart card has only one chip embedded in it the chip is known as a monochip. The term usually refers to a single chip which has both processing ability (the microprocessor) and memory.

non-volatile memory   Memory which retains its contents when power is removed.

open zone   The area of a smart card's memory where non-confidential information is stored.

operating system   Program which supervises and sequences other programs, and sometimes incorporates commonly used functions e.g. send data to read/write units. The operating system is not dependent upon the application.

optical memory card   Also known as a laser card. A technology similar to that used for optical discs. A laser is used to burn holes in a reflective material on the card. The presence, or absence, of a hole represents the binary digits 1 and 0. Data is read using a laser which picks out the non-reflective areas exposed during the recording process. It is a non-rewritable memory with its major feature being that its capacity is as great as 2 megabytes.

outer lead bonding   Process used in tape automated bonding which connects conducting tape, attached to the bonding pads of a chip, to the conducting tracks of a substrate on which the chip is to be mounted.

personal computer (PC)   Desk-top computer which incorporates a display and a keyboard. Often referred to as a PC.

personal identification number (PIN)   Number assigned to a card holder which is used by the cardholder to verify to a system that he or she can legitimately use the card.

personalisation   Storage in the smart card of details relating to the individual to whom the card is to belong, for example name, address, PIN.

photolithography   Process for transferring circuit patterns on to a chip or board (substrate) during manufacture.

pin pad   Keyboard which allows a cardholder to enter a personal identification number into a system.

Prestel   An information service, supplying sports, travel, share and other information, provided by British Telecom and which the general public can access with the appropriate equipment. Charges are made for the use of this service.

private key   See **secret key.**

program   The instructions stored in memory which define precisely the operations a smart card or computer or microcomputer is to perform and the sequence in which the operations are to be performed.

programmable read-only memory (PROM)   Memory which can be programmed and which retains its contents when power is removed.

public key   In an encryption system, such as RSA, in which it is not necessary to keep both the encryption and decryptions keys secret to maintain security, the key that can be published and made generally available is known as the public key.

radio frequency identification (RF/ID)   The transmission method most frequently used by tags is radio frequency and the complete system, incorporating tags and the interrogator/reader, is known as radio frequency identification.

random access memory (RAM)   Memory whose contents can both be read and written to in any order. When electrical power is removed data stored in RAM is lost and, for this reason, it is usually used for temporary storage. In some cards, usually memory cards thicker than the ISO standard, RAM is used as the principal memory but, in these cases, a battery is incorporated in the card so that the memory contents can be retained when the card is removed from the read/write unit.

read-only memory (ROM)   Non-volatile memory whose contents can only be read. The contents of the ROM are embedded in the ROM at the chip manufacturing stage.

read/write unit   The unit through which a smart card communicates with other devices. It provides the power necessary for the smart card to operate and is the means for writing data into the card or reading data from the card.

RSA   An encryption method, named after the initials of its inventors, Rivest, Shamir and Adleman. The RSA method of encryption is known as a public key encryption method because it is not necessary to keep both the encryption and decryption keys secret – one can be published.

RS-232 interface   Standard electrical connection interface in which all the leads are defined. A common standard for serial data communications. Many of today's personal computers have an RS-232 socket for the connection of external devices.

scanner   See **interrogator.**

secret key   In a public key encryption system only one of the keys – the encryption key or the decryption key – must be kept secret. This key is known as the secret key or the private key.

secret zone   That part of a smart card's memory containing completely confidential information which is not accessible to the cardholder and need not be known in total to the card manufacturer or issuer. This area of memory holds such data as the PIN.

smart card   Computer in a bank credit card type package, typically, £5 large quantities.

software   The set of instructions (program) and data stored in the memory of a smat card or computer/microcomputer which causes it to perform a particular task.

solar cell   Device which generates electrical power when light falls on it.

substrate   The small board on which the chip or chips are mounted prior to embedding in a smart card. The substrate can be flexible or rigid, is an electrical insulating material and contains the electrically conducting tracks which connect the chips to the surface contacts of the smart card – or, in a contactless smart card, to other parts of the circuit such as the aerial coil.

super smart card   Smart card with integrated keyboard and display.

tag   Small electronic module, available in various sizes and shapes, which transmits identification information or other data over a range from a few millimetres up to several metres. Radio frequency is the most common means of transmission used. As the name implies, tags are usually used for tracking and identification, for example tracking articles on a production line. Sometimes referred to as the transponder.

tape automated bonding (TAB)   Method of connecting the outer pads of a chip to other parts of a circuit or to external contacts. Tape with conducting tracks is used to make the connection rather than thin wire which is the traditional connecting medium.

thermode   Tool which applies heat and pressure to allow inner lead and outer lead bonds to be made in the tape automated bonding process.

transponder   See **tag.**

viewdata   General term used for an information service such as Prestel or Teletext. See also **Prestel.**

volatile memory   Memory which loses its contents when power is removed.

wafer   Silicon disc, typically 5in in diameter and 0.2in thick, which undergoes various processes that result in it ending as a disc comprising a number of chips. The wafer is later sawn up into individual chips.

watermark   Technique, developed by EMI/Malco, which provides a magnetic stripe with a higher level of security. The card's unique serial number is incorporated in the magnetic stripe in a machine-readable form. The number on the stripe must match the number on the card before the machine will accept it.

wire bonding   Commonly used method, in the chip industry, of connecting, with thin wire, the chip pads (outer connections of the chip) to a circuit or to the external contacts of the package in which the chip is eventually encapsulated.

working zone   The area of a smart card's memory which contains confidential information which can only be read after the cardholder has identified himself, usually via a PIN.

APPENDIX: SMART CARD SUPPLIERS AND USERS

Company	Telephone No.	Status
AT&T 295 N. Maple Avenue, Room 6156H2, Basking Ridge, NJ07929, USA,	+1 201 221 3690	Supplier
Applied Systems Institute 1420 K Street NW, Suite 400, Washington DC, 20005, USA	+1 202 371 1600	User/ Supplier
Arimura Institute of Technology 21-32 Sai Wai-cho, Chigasaki City, Kanawaga Prefecture, Japan	+81 467 87 0114	Supplier
Asset Card Ltd. Level Four, Chase House, 50 Anzac Avenue, Private Bag 1, Auckland, New Zealand	+64 9 773 300	User
Bank of America 45 S Hudson Street, Pasadena, CA91101, USA	+1 818 578 5457	User

Barclaycard	+44 604 252616	User
Barclaycard Centre		
Northampton, NN1 1SG, England		
Bull CP8	+33 1 30 69 50	Supplier
rue Eugene Henaff BP54,		
78193 Trappes Cedex, France		
California State Lottery	+1 916 323 8068	User
600 N 10th Street,		
Sacramento, CA95814, USA		
Catalyst Semiconductor Inc.	+1 408 748 7700	Supplier
2231 Calle de Luna,		
Santa Clara, CA95054, USA		
Crouzet SA	+1 212 230 3258	Supplier
885 Third Avenue, Suite 2911,		
New York, NY10022, USA		
Crouzet SA	+33 75 55 41 00	Supplier
Division Terminaux et Systemes,		
25 rue Jules Vedrines,		
26027 Valence Cedex, France		
Dai Nippon Printing Co. Ltd.	+1 212 686 1919	Supplier
2 Park Avenue, 14th Floor,		
New York, NY10016, USA		
Dai Nippon Printing Co. Ltd.	+81 3 266 2563	Supplier
1-1 Ichigaya Kagacho, 1-chome,		
Shinjuku-ku, Tokyo, Japan		
Datakey, Inc.	+1 612 890 6850	Supplier
12281 Nicollet Avenue,		
Burnsville, MN55337, USA		
De La Rue Co.	+44 1 734 8020	Supplier
De La Rue House,		
3-5 Burlington Gardens,		
London, W1A 1DL, England		
Deutsche Bundespost	+49 911 4328263	User
Fernmeldetechnisches Zentralamt,		
Gibitzenhofstrasse 84,		
POB 100012 Nurnberg, 8500,		
FR Germany		
Drexler Technology Corp.	+1 415 969 7277	Supplier
2557 Charleston Road,		
Mountain View, CA94043, USA		
EM Microelectronic-Marin SA	+41 38 35 21 2	Supplier
CH-2074 Marin, Switzerland		

EyeDentify Inc. PO Box 3827, Portland, OR97208, USA	+1 503 645 0567	Supplier
Farco Collison House, 58-60 Coventry Road, Coleshill, W Midlands, B46 3EE, England	+44 675 467170	Supplier
Farco SA Girardet 55, CH-2400 Le Locle, Switzerland	+41 39 31 89 54	Supplier
Fingermatrix Inc. 30 Virginia Road, N White Plains, NY10603-2297, USA	+1 914 428 5441	Supplier
France Telecom 20 avenue de Segur, 75007 Paris, France		User
Fujitsu Ltd. 1405 Ohmaru, Inagi, Tokyo 100, Japan	+81 423 77 4111	Supplier
Fujitsu Micro Electronics Inc. 3545 N First Street, San Jose, CA95134, USA	+1 408 922 9000	Supplier
Fujitsu Microelectronics Ltd. Hargrave House, Belmont Road, Maidenhead, Berkshire, SL6 6NE, England	+44 628 76100	Supplier
GEC Card Technology Woodruff Way, Tame Bridge, Walsall, W Midlands, WS5 4AE, England	+44 21 555 6280	Supplier
Gemplus Card International 15 avenue Camille-Pelletan, BP 648, Aix-en-Provence, Cedex 2, 13094, France	+33 42 60 30 02	Supplier
Groupe Segin rue de la Pointe, 59113 Seclin, France	+33 20 32 02 52	Supplier
Groupement des Cartes Bancaires (CB) 29 rue de Lisbonne, 75008 Paris, France	+33 142 89 2121	Supplier
Hitachi Electronic Components Ltd. 21 Upton Road, Watford, Hertfordshire, WD1 7TB, England	+44 923 246488	Supplier

Hitachi Ltd.		Supplier
6 Kanda-surugadai, 4-chome,		
Chiyoda-ku, Tokyo 101		
Japan		
Hitachi Maxell Ltd.	+81 3 241 9321	Supplier
Takeda Honcho Bldg,		
2-1-7 Nihonbashi Honcho, Chuo-ku,		
Tokyo, 103, Japan		
Honeywell Bull Ltd.	+44 442 232222	Supplier
Maxted Road, Hemel Hempstead,		
Hertfordshire, HP2 7DZ, England		
Identix Inc.	+1 408 739 3308	Supplier
510 N Pastoria Avenue,		
Sunnyvale, CA94086, USA		
Logicam	+33 142 40 9574	Supplier
39 Boulevard Magenta,		
75010 Paris, France		
Logicard Systems Inc.	+1 914 769 1400	Supplier
401 Columbus Avenue,		
Valhalla, NY10595, USA		
MasterCard International	+1 212 649 5450	User
888 Seventh Avenue,		
New York, NY10106, USA		
Matsushita Electric Industrial	+81 6 908 1121	Supplier
1006 Kadoma, Kadoma City,		
Osaka, 571, Japan		
Maxell Corp. of America	+1 201 794 5900	Supplier
22-08 Route 208,		
Fair Lawn, NJ07410, USA		
Maxell Europe GmbH	+49 211 59510	Supplier
Am Seestern 24,		
4000 Duesseldorf 11, FR Germany		
Micro Card Technologies Inc.	+1 214 788 4055	Supplier
14070 Proton Road, Dallas,		
TX75244, USA		
Midland Bank plc	+44 1 260 6161	User
Payment Services Division,		
59 Gracechurch Street,		
London, EC3V 0JH, England		
Mitsubishi Electric Corp.	+44 7072 76100	Supplier
Kita-Itami Works F4-1 Mizuhara,		
Itami City 664, Hyogo, Japan		

Mitsubishi Electric UK Ltd.		Supplier
Travellers Lane, Hatfield,		
Hertfordshire, AL10 8XB, England		
Mitsubishi Electronics	+1 408 730 5900	Supplier
Semiconductor Division,		
1050 E Arques Avenue,		
Sunnyvale, CA94086, USA		
Monedata	+33 147 78 7473	Supplier
4 rue des Courrières,		
92000 Nanterre, France		
Motorola	+1 512 440 2093	Supplier
William Cannon 290 W,		
PO Box 6000, Austin,		
TX78762, USA		
Motorola Inc.	+41 22 799 1111	Supplier
European Semiconductor Group,		
16 Chemin de la Voie-Creuse,		
CH-1211 Geneva 20, Switzerland		
Motorola Ltd.	+44 3552 39101	Supplier
Colvilles Road, Kelvin Estate,		
East Kilbride, Glasgow,		
G75 0TG, Scotland		
Multimil Inc.	+1 214 644 7724	Supplier
670 International Parkway,		
Suite 190, Richardson,		
TX75081, USA		
Multimil International SA	+41 22 47 52 55	Supplier
12 Chemin Rieu, CH-1208,		
Geneva, Switzerland		
NEC	+81 3 454 1111	Supplier
5-33-1 Shiba, Minato-ku,		
Tokyo, 108, Japan		
NTT	+81 3 509 3051	Supplier
1-1-6 Uchi-saiwa icho,		
Chiyoda-ku, Tokyo, 100, Japan		
National Physical Laboratory	+44 1 977 3222	Supplier
Teddington, Middlesex,		
TW11 0LW, England		
Nippon LSI Card Co. Ltd.	+81 6 789 2226	Supplier
8 Takaida Higashi 2-chome,		
Higashi-Osaka 577, Japan		
Oki America Inc.	+1 212 972 8410	Supplier
575 Fifth Avenue, Floor 19,		
New York City, NY10017, USA		

Oki Electric Europe GmbH Niederkasseler Lohweg 8, D-4000 Duesseldorf 11, FR Germany	+49 211 59 55 0	Supplier
Personal Computer Card Corp. 805 Third Avenue, Sixth Floor, New York, NY10022, USA	+1 212 355 4334	Supplier
Philips International BV PO Box 245, Apeldoorn NL-7300 AE, Netherlands	+31 55 43 24 39	Supplier
Philips TDS Bus Group Smart Card 4-16 Avenue du General LeClerc, Fontenay-aux-Roses, 92660, France	+33 1 470 26 32	Supplier
Royal Bank of Canada 180 Wellington Street W, Toronto, ONT, M5J 1J1, Canada	+1 416 974 4142	User
Sanshin & Co. Ltd. Ota Building 25-7, Sanei-cho, Shinjuku-ku, Tokyo, 160, Japan	+81 3 225 9091	Supplier
Schlumberger CMS Systemes de Paiement, 420 rue d'Estienne d'Orves, BP 84, Colombes, 92704, France	+33 147 80 7181	Supplier
Segin rue de la Pointe, Z.1-59113 Seclin, France	+33 20 32 02 52	Supplier
Siemens AG Dept DVMP144, PO 830451, Otto Hamn Ring No. 6, D-8000 Munich, FR Germany	+49 89636 44758	Supplier
Sligos Payment Systems Division, 3 Place de la Pyramide, 92067 Paris La Defense, Cedex 49, France	+33 149 00 9000	Supplier
Smart Card International Inc. 404 Park Avenue S, New York, NY10016, USA	+1 212 481 3700	Supplier

Smart Card International Inc.	+ 44 689 78345	Supplier
Refuge House,		
217-9 High Street,		
Orpington, Kent,		
BR6 0NZ, England		
Solaic	+33 149 00 9000	Supplier
Cedex 49,		
92067 Paris La Defense, France		
Thomas Cook Group Ltd.	+44 733 50 2104	Supplier
PO Box 36, Thorpe Wood,		
Peterborough, PE3 6SB, England		
Thomson Components Ltd.	+44 256 23172	Supplier
Ringway House, Bell Road,		
Daneshill, Basingstoke,		
Hampshire, RG24 0QG, England		
Thomson Components (Mostek Corp.)	+1 214 466 6000	Supplier
1310 Electronics Drive,		
Carrollton, TX75006, USA		
Thomson Semiconducteurs	+33 139 46 9719	Supplier
43 Avenue de l'Europe,		
78140 Paris-Velizy, France		
Toppan Printing Co. Ltd.	+81 3 835 5111	Supplier
1 Kanda Izumicho,		
Chiyoda-ku, Tokyo, 101, Japan		
Toshiba	+81 3 457 4511	Supplier
1-1-1 Shibaura,		
Minato-ku, Tokyo,		
105-01, Japan		
Toshiba America Inc.	+1 714 583 3275	Supplier
9740 Irvine Boulevard,		
Irvine, CA92718, USA		
US Department of Agriculture	+1 202 382 0205	User
Agricultural Stabilization & Cons. Serv.,		
PO Box 2415, Washington DC,		
20013, USA		
UWIST Welsh School of Pharmacy	+44 222 42588	User
King Edward VII Avenue,		
Cardiff, CF1 3NU, Wales		
Valvo	+49 40 3296 222	Supplier
Burchardstrasse 19,		
2000 Hamburg 1, FR Germany		

Visa International PO Box 253, London, W8 5GE, England	+44 1 937 8111	User
Visa International PO Box 8999, San Francisco, CA94018, USA	+1 415 570 3785	User

Index